THE SCREEN PLAYBOOK:

A Writer's Guide to Negotiating Creative Rights Like a Pro

TISHA MORRIS, ESQ.

The Screen Playbook: A Writer's Guide to Negotiating Creative Rights Like a Pro

Legacy Arts Publishing LLC

Book Interior, Book Cover and E-book Design by Amit Dey

ISBN: 978-1-953596-27-7 (paperback)
ISBN: 978-1-953596-28-4 (eBook)

Dedicated to the creatives who believe stories have the power to move hearts, shift culture, and bring light into the world.

DISCLAIMER

As you might expect from a book written by an attorney, this book starts with a disclaimer:

The information contained in this book is provided for general informational and educational purposes only and is not intended as, and should not be construed as, legal advice. The contents reflect the author's general observations about the entertainment industry and the legal frameworks that govern it, but every legal matter is fact-specific, and the application of any legal principle discussed in this book to a particular situation requires the analysis of a qualified attorney familiar with the facts of that situation and the law of the relevant jurisdiction.

Reading this book does not create an attorney-client relationship between the reader and the author, between the reader and Tisha Morris, Esq., or between the reader and any law firm or attorney with whom the author is or has been associated. No attorney-client relationship is formed by the purchase, receipt, or review of this book, by any communication directed to the author in connection with this book, or by any other interaction arising from this book in the absence of a separately executed written engagement agreement.

The laws governing copyright, contracts, intellectual property, and the entertainment industry are complex, vary by jurisdiction, and change over time. Statutes are amended, regulations are revised, and the courts continue to interpret and reinterpret existing law. The information in this book reflects the author's understanding as of the date of writing and is not a substitute for current legal research or for the advice of a licensed attorney in the reader's jurisdiction. Before entering into any agreement, signing any document, or taking any action based on the topics discussed in this book, the reader should consult with a qualified attorney who can evaluate the reader's specific circumstances.

The author and publisher disclaim any and all liability arising directly or indirectly from the use or application of any information contained in this book. Examples, scenarios, and case discussions are illustrative only. Any resemblance to actual persons, transactions, or disputes, except where specifically identified by reference to a published court decision, is either coincidental or composed for instructional purposes.

If you are involved in or contemplating an entertainment industry transaction, dispute, or other legal matter, retain qualified counsel.

TABLE OF CONTENTS

OPENING SCENE

INTRODUCTION

I want you to succeed and fulfill your greatest dreams through your creative work. And to do that, you need to know the business side of the craft. Writing the script or the book is only the beginning. The real journey begins when you, or someone else, wants to turn your work into something more. That's where the business side comes in.

Great projects fail every day for reasons that have nothing to do with the work itself. Instead, they fail because the writer signed a shopping agreement that tied up the project for years. They fail because the underlying rights weren't cleared and the chain of title can't be insured. They fail because the writer agreed to a backend definition that paid out at zero on a film that grossed a hundred million dollars. None of these examples are about talent. These failures are about the business behind the creative work, and each one of them is preventable once you know how to navigate it.

Most books written for writers don't cover the business side. They teach you how to be a good writer. But there's a gap when your script stops being a creative document and starts being an asset that other people want to acquire, control, and exploit. This book is meant to close that gap between your creative talents and business acumen. By the end, you'll know how to protect your work and negotiate from a position of understanding with the people who want to acquire and exploit it.

My goal is to give you the tools to know when you need representation, to spot issues before they become problems, to recognize when you're being represented well, and to feel confident as a creative. I've gathered the most common scenarios and documents you'll come across, along with the questions I most often get, and translated them out of legalese into plain English.

My own entry into the entertainment industry as an attorney came through the creative side as an author. When working with clients or handling transactions, I keep the creative person at the center of it. It's from that perspective I wrote this book. It's for the writer, filmmaker, showrunner, producer, novelist, and entrepreneur who wants to remain a creative while maximizing the potential of their project, building a career, and succeeding without being taken advantage of in the process.

This book is structured like a screenplay in Acts with each covering a phase of a project's commercial life in the order in which a working writer may likely encounter such transactions. At the beginning of each Act is a real-life narrative to give context and shape to the chapters ahead. Each of these scenarios is one I've seen firsthand, most often in the form of a client who came to me for legal representation one bad deal too late. The goal is to act proactively before you become one of these all-too-common cautionary tales.

Act I: Owning the Story starts where every deal begins, which is with the question of what you actually own. Issues around copyright, source material, fair use, chain of title are all discussed, including a step-by-step guide on how to file a copyright.

Act II: Enter the Dealmaker is about the mindset shift that every creative must make by putting on the business hat, understanding leverage, and learning to think about your creative work as the asset it has now become.

Act III: Getting the Project Off the Ground addresses the development phase in which a project moves from a finished script toward a producible film or series. This is the phase where representation, pitching, producers, and the early foundation of a deal first appear and where the choices you make begin to compound.

Act IV: The Agreements That Drive the Industry is the heart of the book in terms of the documents you will sign. Shopping agreements, option agreements, option-purchase agreements, literary purchase agreements, licenses, assignments, life rights, and other agreements through which rights move from the writer to the producer and onward are differentiated and distinguished from one another, since they often overlap in confusing ways.

Act V: Negotiating the Deal covers the details where economics and control are determined in the form of price, term, territory, exclusivity, backend participation, credit, and reversion. These are the deal points that determine how much you are paid, how long the other side holds your rights, and what happens if the project succeeds beyond anyone's expectations or, on the other end of the spectrum, never gets made at all.

Act VI: The Fine Print covers the provisions that every exhausted party at the end of a long negotiation is tempted to treat as boilerplate, including force majeure, warranties and indemnification, choice of law, and dispute resolution. They look like standard language right up until they decide the outcome of a dispute. At that point, these provisions become the only language that matters.

The book closes with a summary of the most common terms used in the industry with context for the language used in financing the film, development, and production. The Final Scene of the book walks the reader through steps on how to practically build and maintain a sustainable career in an industry built on IP.

The chapters that follow are written to be read in order, but each section is also meant to function as a reference you can return to when you encounter a specific transaction or document for the first time.

The intent is not for you to memorize everything in this book, but to familiarize yourself with the business cycle of a script-to-screen project so you can recognize these transactions when they show up across the table and know what questions to ask. Although the book is in no way exhaustive of all the legal documents or industry jargon you may encounter, you will walk away feeling much more confident in navigating the business side of being a creative than when you began.

Also included throughout are *Pro Tips* to give you a real-world advantage in navigating the entertainment industry. These are points I've learned along the way as an entertainment attorney that they don't teach you in film school (or in law school) but are here to help you leverage your creative career as much as possible. The more structures you have in place on the business side, the better you can feel about creating your next project knowing you have the foundations in place to position it favorably.

Let's begin.

ACT I

Owning the Story

A producer had optioned Mara's screenplay eighteen months earlier. It was a drama based on a long-form magazine article she had discovered and loved. It read like fiction, and she had known from the first paragraph it should be a film. She had adapted it carefully, submitted it through her manager, and signed the option agreement the same week it arrived. She had not asked an attorney to review it. Her manager was enthusiastic and the option check cleared within the week.

The producer's email was brief, but the gist of it was the project had found financing. A director was attached and the studio wanted to move into pre-production within sixty days. There was, however, a problem. The studio's business affairs team had conducted a rights clearance review and discovered that the magazine article Mara had adapted was itself based on a published memoir, still under copyright, held by an estate that had not been contacted, had not been compensated, and had not authorized any adaptation of any kind. The screenplay Mara had spent eight months writing did not have a clean chain of title.

The project did not fall apart, but it came close. Negotiating a retroactive life rights agreement with the estate took four months and a significant payment that no one budgeted for. In the meantime, the director moved on and the financing shrank. The version of the film that eventually got made was a diminished version of the one that had been greenlit, and Mara spent two years wondering what might have happened if she'd taken the right steps at the beginning.

CHAPTER 1

INTELLECTUAL PROPERTY

Before you can negotiate a deal, sign an agreement, or engage a producer in any meaningful conversation about your project, you need to understand what you own and what you don't own. That inquiry begins and ends with a single concept: intellectual property.

What Is Intellectual Property?

Intellectual property is referred to throughout this book, as it is throughout the industry, as "IP." This is the legal term for tangible creations that the law recognizes as protectable assets. IP is the foundation upon which every entertainment deal is built. It is the thing being bought, licensed, optioned, or assigned. It is the subject of your chain of title. It is what the producer is paying for, what the studio is acquiring, and what you may find yourself losing if not careful.

Intellectual property law in the United States and throughout most of the world recognizes three primary categories: trademarks, patents, and copyrights. Each protects a different kind of creative or commercial asset, and each operates under its own legal framework. A writer entering a negotiation does not need to be an expert in all three. But you do need to understand their distinctions not to confuse them, since doing so could expose you to liability you did not know you were assuming.

The following sections will describe each type of IP starting with patents, which is the least important to writers, followed by trademarks, and finally the most important IP for writers: copyright.

Patents

A patent is a government-granted right that allows an inventor to exclude others from making, using, or selling an invention for a defined period of time. Patents protect functional inventions and novel processes. They are the domain of engineers, pharmaceutical companies, and technology developers. For most screenwriters, novelists, and other creative professionals whose work this book addresses, patents are essentially irrelevant. You will not patent your screenplay. No one will seek to patent your plot. In fact, it is not customary for entertainment attorneys to handle patent applications at all. Patents are simply mentioned here to round out the explanation of what IP is.

Trademarks

A trademark is a word, phrase, symbol, logo, or combination thereof that identifies and distinguishes the source of goods or services in commerce. The Nike "Swoosh." The Warner Brother's shield. The phrase "Netflix Original." These are trademarks. Trademark law is primarily concerned with preventing consumer confusion about the origin of commercial products and services. It protects brand identity, not creative content.

For most writers, trademarks are a peripheral concern rather than a central one. You may encounter trademark issues if your script features a real brand prominently enough to suggest endorsement or affiliation that does not exist, or if a title you have chosen for your project is confusingly similar to an existing trademark in the entertainment space. But trademarks do not protect the story you wrote. They do not protect your dialogue or your narrative structure. That protection comes from an entirely different body of law.

Trademarks, however, can and often do intersect with the business of entertainment. For example, a production company that develops a recognizable brand over time, a book series whose title has acquired commercial distinctiveness in the marketplace, a fictional character whose name and visual identity have become independently associated with a particular creative universe each may be protectable as a trademark, independently of and in addition to whatever copyright protection attaches to the underlying creative work.

The distinction matters because copyright and trademark protect different things and expire on different schedules. Copyright in a novel eventually enters the public domain; trademark rights in the title of that novel's series, if properly maintained and continuously used in commerce, may endure indefinitely. A character whose copyright protection is uncertain because of age, authorship complications, or the work-for-hire doctrine may nonetheless carry trademark rights that restrict how the character's name and distinctive visual elements can be commercially exploited by third parties.

The practical implications arise in cases when a writer, producer, or production entity is building something intended to function as a brand, such as a recurring franchise, a titled series with sequel potential, a production company whose name will appear on multiple projects over time, or a character whose commercial identity may eventually extend into merchandising, licensing, and ancillary exploitation.

A more recent use of trademarks is for AI characters that would otherwise not be subject to copyright protection under current copyright law. The United States Copyright Office requires copyrights to be human created, which will be discussed in more detail in the chapter that follows. However, a character completely created by AI, so long as it is used in commerce could be filed successfully as a trademark.

A full analysis of trademark law, including clearance searches, registration strategy, likelihood-of-confusion analysis, and the maintenance obligations that attach to a registered mark, is beyond the scope of this book. It is best to consult with an intellectual property attorney at the outset of building anything intended to function as a brand to avoid costly disputes that could arise down the road.

Copyrights

Copyright is the form of intellectual property protection that governs literary, artistic, and creative works. As a writer, this is the category that has direct application to your career. A screenplay is a copyrighted work. A novel is a copyrighted work. The treatment you wrote, the short story on which your script is based, the original song featured in your film are all copyrighted works. Every entertainment deal, at its core, is a transaction in copyright. When a producer options a script, they are acquiring the temporary right to exploit the copyright. When a studio purchases a screenplay, they are acquiring ownership of that copyright outright. When a television network licenses a format, they are licensing rights derived from your copyright. When a publisher publishes a book, they are licensing the copyright from the author to do so. The deal points we will examine in detail throughout this book are all mechanisms by which copyright interests are allocated, transferred, or retained.

The next chapter addresses copyright law in considerably more depth, including what it protects, how it arises, how long it lasts, and the critically misunderstood doctrine of fair use. For now, the foundational point is that under United States copyright law, a work is protected by copyright from the moment it is created and fixed in a tangible medium of expression. You do not need to register your work to own the copyright. You do not need to affix a copyright notice. The act of writing the script, saving the document, printing the pages is sufficient to establish copyright protection as a matter of law. However, registration, which will be discussed in detail, carries significant legal and practical advantages.

Who Owns the Copyright?

If you wrote it, you own it. It's (almost always) that simple. As the author of an original creative work, the copyright in that work belongs to you by operation of law. This is also the case with a photographer, graphic designer, painter, software coder, and other creatives. Short of an agreement saying otherwise, you own your creations. That said, the situation is not always so clear. Copyright ownership becomes complicated and disputes arise in several circumstances that writers commonly encounter of which you should be aware.

Co-Written Works

If you wrote your script or other creative work with a collaborator such as a writing partner, a co-author, or a friend who contributed substantially to the story, then you may have created what copyright law calls a "joint work." A joint work is a work prepared by two or more authors with the intention that their contributions be merged into inseparable or interdependent parts of a unitary whole. The legal consequences of joint authorship are significant, especially for writers who did not anticipate them. In fact, you may have unintentionally entered into a partnership under the law without realizing it.

Under U.S. copyright law, each co-author of a joint work is a co-owner of the entire copyright, not just their portion of it. Also important to know is that each co-owner has the right to exploit the work, license it to third parties, or authorize its use without the consent of the other co-owners. They do however have an obligation to account for and share any resulting profits. Yes, that means your writing partner can, without your permission, license your jointly written screenplay to a producer, grant an option to a studio, or authorize a derivative work. They must share the income with you, but they do not need your approval. If you're thinking that this could create a real problem in the industry, then you're right.

The solution is a written co-authorship or collaboration agreement executed at the outset of any collaborative project, preferably before the first draft is written. That agreement should address, at minimum, each writer's ownership percentage, the decision-making authority required to license, sell, or otherwise exploit the work, how writing credit will be allocated, and what happens if one co-author wants to exit the collaboration or dies. Collaboration agreements will be discussed in more detail later, but for now, know that if you co-wrote your script, you do not unilaterally own the copyright. And if you have not documented the terms of your collaboration in writing, you have created a joint work and a potential dispute awaiting you down the road.

PRO TIP:

Email communications can create a contract and therefore be evidence for agreed upon terms between two writers. However, a formal agreement is recommended to avoid the cost of litigating the email exchanges, not to mention deal points not included in the email exchanges.

The Acquired Material

The other common complication arises when your project is based on, adapted from, or derived from material that someone else created; for example, a screenplay based on a published novel, a biopic drawn from a journalist's investigative article, or a limited series adapted from a true-crime podcast. In each of these cases, the underlying material in the form of a novel, article, or podcast is itself a copyrighted work—owned by someone else. Before you can legally exploit your screenplay, you need the rights to the underlying material. Before you can grant a producer the right to produce your script, you need to be able to represent that you have cleared the rights that allow you to do so. This is the concept at the heart of what the industry calls "chain of title."

Chain of title is the documented, unbroken sequence of ownership and rights transfers that establishes that the party selling or licensing a project has the legal authority to do so. Chain of title begins with the original creator and must, without gap or ambiguity, run to the party currently offering the rights. A broken chain of title, which could be a missing assignment, an undocumented license, or an underlying rights holder who was never approached, is one of the most common reasons entertainment deals collapse at the legal review stage. Studios and distributors require clean chain of title as a condition of closing. Errors and omissions insurers require it as a condition of issuing coverage. If you cannot demonstrate a clean chain of title, your project does not move. You can now begin to understand the importance of copyright ownership.

Every agreement you will encounter in this industry is, at its core, a document that transfers, restricts, or allocates rights in a copyrighted work. The deal points that will consume much of this book, including price, term, territory, backend, and reversion, are all parameters placed around a copyright transaction. When you understand that, you understand why the question of who owns what, and on what basis, must be answered clearly before any other negotiation can proceed.

The copyright is the asset the other side wants. Never enter a negotiation without knowing exactly what you own, how you came to own it, and what, if anything, might complicate that ownership. The chapters that follow will give you the frameworks to make that assessment accurately and to protect what you have built.

CHAPTER 2

COPYRIGHT BASICS FOR CREATIVES

Before getting into the mechanics of copyright law, it's worth noting the intended purpose Congress had in constructing the legislation. Article I, Section 8 of the United States Constitution grants Congress the power to secure "for authors and inventors" the exclusive right to their respective writings and discoveries, and it explicitly states the reason is *to promote the progress of science and the useful arts*.

A copyright gives the creator the ability to control and benefit from one's creative work and, in turn, this is what induces creators to create in the first place. The social bargain embedded in copyright law is that society benefits from the continuous production of new creative works, and creators benefit from the legal infrastructure that makes those works worth producing. This framework is in essence the spirit behind copyright law.

As such, copyright law is a federal statutory framework that grants the creator of an original work a bundle of exclusive rights in that work, which includes the rights to reproduce it, distribute it, prepare derivative works based upon it, and publicly display or perform it. The governing statute is the Copyright Act of 1976, codified at Title 17 of the United States Code, and it is, well let's say, not beach reading. But you do not need to master the statute to understand why it matters to you. The first thing to know is that your screenplay, book, the note you wrote to your girlfriend, or any other written work is a copyrighted work the moment it is fixed in a "tangible medium of expression." That means the moment you put anything on paper, on a computer, on someone's arm, or anywhere physical and tangible, you have a copyright. No registration is required. The copyright belongs to you by operation of law.

Simple, right? The more complicated part however is that copyright is not a single, indivisible right. It is a bundle of rights, each of which can be transferred independently, licensed exclusively or nonexclusively, retained in whole or in part, and encumbered in ways that are not always visible on the surface of a deal. Understanding that bundle, and how each component of it functions in the context of an entertainment transaction, is the foundational prerequisite to understanding every agreement you will ever sign in the industry.

Copyright Protection

Copyright protects the expression of an idea—not the idea itself. This distinction, sometimes called the idea-expression dichotomy, is one of the most frequently misunderstood concepts in copyright law that carries over into the entertainment industry. You cannot copyright the premise of a fish-out-of-water comedy. You cannot copyright the concept of a heist told in reverse chronology. You cannot copyright the theme of redemption, the archetype of the reluctant hero, or the three-act structure. What you can copyright is the specific, original expression of those ideas as embodied in your script in the form of your dialogue, your scene descriptions, your character names and backstories, the particular sequence and arrangement of scenes and story beats that constitute your work.

This means your copyright does not prevent someone else from writing a different script about, say, a disgraced attorney who returns to his hometown to save a family farm. It prevents them from copying your script about that attorney. Second, and conversely, it means that when you adapt source material, i.e. a novel, a news article, a podcast, a true story, the copyright in your screenplay covers your expression, not the underlying material. Those are separate intellectual properties, and managing the relationship between them is one of the primary challenges we will address in the chapters on chain of title and underlying rights.

Registration and Why You Should

Although copyright protection arises automatically upon fixation, registration with the United States Copyright Office is a professional non-negotiable. Under 17 U.S.C. § 411, you generally cannot file a lawsuit for copyright infringement until you have registered your work. More significantly, under 17 U.S.C. § 412, if your work was not registered prior to the infringement, or within three months of first publication, then you are ineligible for statutory damages and attorney's fees. You are limited to actual damages, which are notoriously difficult to prove and often insufficient to justify the cost of litigation. For this reason alone, copyright registration is cannot be replicated by other methods you may have heard about, for example, mailing yourself a copy, a date stamp on your computer, or even filing with the WGA office.

In practical terms, a writer who circulates a script without registering it first has significantly reduced leverage in the event of a dispute. Registration costs a modest filing fee and is completed online through the Copyright Office portal, which is explained in more detail in the sections to come.

PRO TIP:

Register your work at www.copyright.gov before submitting to third parties.

Although a copyright is automatically created the moment an original work of authorship is fixed in a tangible medium of expression, registering your copyright creates a public record of your claim to ownership. It is a documented, timestamped assertion, filed with the United States Copyright Office, that you are the author of a particular work and that you claim the rights to that authorship.

A registered copyright is searchable in the Copyright Office's public records. A producer, studio, or financier conducting due diligence on a project can locate the registration, confirm authorship, and trace the recorded history of any transfers or licenses. This is essential when it comes to chain of title purposes. An unregistered copyright is not searchable in that way. While its existence can be asserted through evidence, it cannot be readily verified, nor will it be subject to the statutory damages for which a registration allows. For a writer seeking to establish clean title in a commercial transaction, registration is imperative.

Works Subject to Copyright Protection

Before proceeding to the mechanics of registration, it is worth establishing precisely what kinds of works are eligible for copyright protection. The Copyright Act protects "original works of authorship fixed in any tangible medium of expression." That formulation encompasses a wide range of creative material. Copyright law identifies eight categories of protectable works. While the categories cover works outside of the scope of entertainment, such as code, software, and website copy, among other things, the categories below are described in terms of their relevance for working in the entertainment industry:

- Literary works, which include not only novels and short stories but also screenplays, teleplays, stage plays, treatments, outlines, and any other written narrative work. A screenplay is a literary work under the Copyright Act. So is a pitch document, a series bible, and a step outline.

- Motion pictures and other audiovisual works, which include completed films, television programs, web series, and any other work consisting of a series of related images intended to be shown by a machine or device. The underlying screenplay is a literary work; the film made from it is an audiovisual work. These are distinct copyrights, and they can be owned by different parties.
- Musical works, including any accompanying words, which covers songs, scores, and any music composed for use in a film or television production. The music heard in a film is typically governed by a synchronization license; the underlying composition is a separate copyright from the sound recording of the performance.
- Sound recordings, which are distinct from the underlying musical works and are copyrighted separately. The performance recorded in the studio is one copyright; the song being performed is another.
- Dramatic works, including any accompanying music, which encompasses stage plays and any work intended to be performed before an audience.
- Pantomimes and choreographic works, which are protectable provided they are fixed in a tangible medium, i.e. described in notation, recorded on film, or otherwise preserved.
- Pictorial, graphic, and sculptural works, which include concept art, storyboards, production design drawings, and any other two- or three-dimensional artistic work. For writers developing visual projects, the artwork created during development may itself constitute a separate copyrightable work.
- Architectural works, which are protected as completed buildings or architectural plans. This category is unlikely to be directly relevant to most writers but is included here for completeness.

What is not protectable is equally important to understand. Ideas, concepts, themes, and plot premises are not copyrightable. Keep in mind that the specific expression of those ideas is protectable, but not the ideas themselves. A writer cannot copyright the concept of a heist film, or the premise of a story set on Mars, or the idea of a protagonist who discovers she was adopted. She can copyright the specific screenplay she wrote expressing those concepts, in all the particularity of its language, structure, and execution. The distinction between idea and expression is among the most litigated issues in copyright law and practically significant for writers navigating claims of similarity between competing projects.

A Step-by-Step Guide to Registering a Copyright

Copyright registration in the United States is administered by the United States Copyright Office, which operates under the Library of Congress. Registration is accomplished through the Copyright Office's online registration system, known as the Electronic Copyright Office, or eCO, accessible at www.copyright.gov. While paper registration remains available for certain categories of works, online registration is faster, less expensive, and produces a searchable public record more efficiently. For most writers, there is no reason to use any other method.

The process is more straightforward than many writers expect. What follows is a step-by-step account of how to register a copyright for a literary work, which is the category most directly applicable to screenplays, teleplays, treatments, and related material. Please note that the steps are in accordance with the procedures as of the date of publication of this book.

Step 1: Create an Account with the Copyright Office. Navigate to copyright.gov and create an account in the eCO system. Avoid any other domains purporting to be a copyright registration portal as those are scams. The process is straightforward and requires only basic identifying information. Once your account is established, you will have access to the registration portal, the ability to track the status of pending applications, and a record of all registrations you have filed under that account. There is no cost to create an account.

Step 2: Initiate a New Registration. From the eCO dashboard, select "Register a New Claim." The system will prompt you to identify the type of work you are registering. For a screenplay or similar written work, select "Literary Work." For a completed film or audiovisual production, select "Work of the Performing Arts" or "Motion Picture/AV Work," depending on the specific nature of the material. If you are uncertain which category applies, the Copyright Office's help documentation provides guidance, and a brief consultation with an entertainment attorney can save you from a misfiled application.

Step 3: Complete the Application. The application requires the following information, each of which you should approach with care and precision:

1. **Title of the work.** Provide the title exactly as it appears on the work itself. If the work is untitled, you may use a descriptive identifier. Avoid abbreviations or informal shorthand that would not appear on the script itself.
2. **Year of creation.** This is the year in which the work was completed in the form you are registering. If you have revised the work substantially since an earlier draft, consider whether a separate registration for the revised version is warranted. A registration of the original protects the original expression; new expression added in revision may require its own registration to be fully protected.
3. **Date and nation of first publication**, if the work has been published. For most unproduced screenplays or unpublished manuscripts, the answer is that the work has not been published, and you should indicate as much. "Publication" in the

copyright sense means the distribution of copies to the public, not simply sharing the script with producers or representatives in the course of development.

4. **Author information.** Identify the author or authors of the work. If the work was created as a work made for hire, meaning it was created by an employee within the scope of employment, or pursuant to a written agreement expressly designating it a work for hire, then the employer or commissioning party is the "author" for copyright purposes, and the application should reflect that. For most independently created screenplays, the writer is the author.
5. **Claimant information.** Claimant information. The claimant is the person or entity claiming copyright ownership at the time of registration. The claimant may be the author, or it may be a different party to whom the author has transferred ownership, for example, a production company that acquired the screenplay by assignment. If rights have been transferred, the application should reflect both the original authorship and the current claimant.
6. **Rights and permissions contact.** This is optional but recommended. Providing contact information for rights inquiries creates a pathway for parties seeking to license or acquire your work to reach you through the public record.

Step 4: Upload the Deposit Copy. The Copyright Office requires you to submit a "deposit copy" of the work being registered, that is, an actual copy of the work, sufficient to identify what is being protected. For most literary works filed online, this means uploading a digital copy of the manuscript or screenplay. The eCO system accepts common file formats, including PDF and Word documents. Upload the most current, complete version of the work in the form you intend to protect.

A few practical points on deposit copies deserve emphasis. First, the deposit copy you submit becomes part of the public record and it is not returned to you. Do not submit a draft that is materially different from the final version of the work. Second, if the screenplay contains material drawn from a copyrighted source, for example, song lyrics embedded in the script, then you should be aware that submitting the deposit copy does not cure any underlying clearance issues with that third-party material. Third, if you are registering a revised version of a previously registered work, the deposit copy should represent the *complete* current version, not merely the new material.

Step 5: Pay the Filing Fee. The Copyright Office charges a filing fee for each registration application. Fee schedules are published on the Copyright Office website and are subject to periodic adjustment; as of the time of writing, the online registration fee for a single work is generally in the range of $65. The eCO system accepts payment by credit card, debit card, or electronic funds transfer. Your application is not complete until payment is processed.

One cost-related note: the Copyright Office also offers a "single application" form for works with a single author who is also the sole claimant and who created a work that is not a work made for hire. This form carries a lower filing fee and a more streamlined process. For most independently written screenplays with a single author, the single application is appropriate and preferable. However, it can also create logistical hurdles in the event of a future assignment of one of the individual works. While the cost savings is tempting, it can be simpler to file separate applications for each work.

Step 6: Await Processing and Receive Your Certificate. Once your application is submitted and payment is processed, the Copyright Office will review the application and, if it is complete and acceptable, issue a certificate of registration. Processing times vary. Online applications are generally processed more quickly than paper applications, but delays are not uncommon, particularly during periods of high volume. As of the time of writing, online applications for literary works are typically processed within several months, though the Copyright Office's website provides current estimated processing times.

Critically, your effective date of registration is the date the Copyright Office receives your complete application, not the date the certificate is issued. This distinction matters for litigation purposes. If you file your application before infringement occurs, you preserve your eligibility for statutory damages and attorney's fees, even if the certificate has not yet been issued when the infringement takes place. Do not wait for the certificate to arrive before relying on your registration in a negotiation or a legal proceeding; the filing date is the operative date. In fact, don't rely on receiving a certificate at all as has been the case with many of my clients.

PRO TIP:

Most publishers file the copyright on behalf of the author upon publishing the work. However, you should always verify that the publishing contract specifies that the publisher is to do so at their expense *in your name* and they actually follow through on doing so.

A Note on WGA Registration

Writers who are members of, or who aspire to work within, the Writers Guild of America are likely familiar with WGA script registration that allows writers to create a dated record of a script's existence by depositing it with the Guild. WGA registration is widely used and has genuine practical utility: it is fast, inexpensive, and provides a credible timestamp that can be useful in establishing priority in a dispute over access to material.

What WGA registration is not, however, is a substitute for federal copyright registration. WGA registration does not confer copyright protection; it does not create a publicly searchable record in the Copyright Office's database; it does not satisfy the registration prerequisite for filing an infringement lawsuit in federal court; and it does not preserve eligibility for statutory damages. It is a useful supplement to federal registration, not a replacement for it. Writers who rely solely on WGA registration under the mistaken belief that it is equivalent to copyright registration are leaving significant legal protections on the table.

Registration with the WGA can be useful for the immediate timestamp and ease of use. However, register with the Copyright Office for the full panoply of legal protections the federal statute provides.

Registration as Professional Discipline

Writers sometimes treat copyright registration as a task to be handled "before the deal closes" or "once the script is really finished." However, registration is most valuable when it is done promptly, before the script enters the marketplace and before any potential infringer has had access to the material.

When a draft is complete enough to be shared with anyone outside your immediate creative circle, register it. The fee is modest in comparison with the protections and peace of mind it will give you. The process, as described above, is simple. And the access to federal courts, eligibility for statutory damages, and a searchable public record of your authorship are protections that no amount of after-the-fact remediation can fully restore once the window has closed.

PRO TIP:

Filing a copyright registration is one thing you can easily do yourself without paying an attorney or third-party service (unlike filing a trademark application).

The Work-for-Hire Exception

For works created on or after January 1, 1978, copyright protection lasts for the life of the author plus seventy years. For works created by multiple authors, the term runs from the death of the last surviving author. These are the default rules with one critical exception and that is the work-made-for-hire doctrine.

Under 17 U.S.C. § 101, a work is a *work made for hire* if it is either (a) created by an employee within the scope of employment, or (b) specially ordered or commissioned pursuant to a written agreement designating it as such, provided it falls within one of several enumerated categories of works, which include contributions to motion pictures and other audiovisual works. When a work qualifies as made for hire, the employer or commissioning party is deemed the legal author for copyright purposes, not the actual author. The copyright term for such works is 95 years from publication or 120 years from creation, whichever expires first, and the writer has no termination rights.

This may arise when a studio hires you to write a screenplay, whether on assignment or in a writer-for-hire deal. Know that the resulting script almost certainly qualifies as a work made for hire. You will be compensated and you may receive credit, but the copyright belongs to the studio from the moment of creation. Every negotiation you will ever have with a studio over an assignment deal takes place against this statutory backdrop. Understanding that you are, in the work-for-hire context, producing an asset for someone else is essential to appreciating why the specific deal terms you negotiate matter so much.

Copyright as the Foundation of Every Deal

Every entertainment transaction is, at its core, a transfer or encumbrance of some portion of a copyright. When a producer options your script, what she is acquiring is the exclusive right, for a defined period, to negotiate for and ultimately purchase your copyright. When a studio buys your screenplay outright, it is acquiring the copyright itself, along with the entire bundle of rights, in perpetuity, throughout the universe, as the standard language invariably puts it. When you license your script for a limited production, you are carving out specific rights from that bundle and granting them for specific purposes while retaining the rest. More on these examples later. For now, know that all deals revolve around the copyright.

This is why a thorough understanding of copyright is a prerequisite to understanding everything else in this book. The concept of chain of title, which will be discussed in Chapter 4, is nothing more than a documented history of how copyright ownership has moved from one party to another over the life of a project. The major deal points that will be analyzed in Act V are all mechanisms for allocating the economic and creative value embedded in a copyright.

CHAPTER 3

THE SOURCE MATERIAL

In the previous chapters, you learned that a copyright is automatically created in any original work of authorship fixed in a tangible medium of expression. Now let's address where the story actually comes from. In the industry, the answer to that question is determined upon what the underlying creative work upon which a film, television series, or other audiovisual production is based. Source material is not a term of art defined in the Copyright Act, but it is one of the most consequential concepts in any entertainment deal because it determines who owns what before any agreement is signed, and therefore who must be brought to the table before production can begin.

The critical principle to understand is if you did not create the underlying copyright, you likely do not have the right to use or adapt it without permission. The right to create a derivative work, which is precisely what an adaptation is, belongs to the copyright owner under 17 U.S.C. § 106(2). Using that material without authorization is infringement. The specific agreements required to clear source material will be addressed in detail in the chapters on rights transactions. For now, it's important to understand what kinds of works serve as source material, what each brings to a deal, and what a writer or producer needs to know before building a project on top of someone else's copyright.

The Original Screenplay

The original screenplay occupies a unique position in that it is the source material. When a writer conceives and executes a wholly original script with characters, story, dialogue, structure, all generated from scratch, there is no underlying rights issue to clear. The writer is the copyright owner, and any deal made with a producer or studio begins and ends with that single copyright. This is the cleanest chain of title scenario in the business, which is part of why original scripts remain attractive to buyers even in an era saturated with IP-driven development. The analysis changes, however, the moment the writer has drawn on any preexisting material in the creation of that script. A character inspired by a real person, a plot borrowed from a news story, or a setting lifted from a novel introduce underlying rights questions that must be resolved before the project can move forward.

Published Novels

The novel is perhaps the second most familiar form of source material in entertainment, and for good reason. It's a commercially successful IP that comes with a built-in audience, a proven narrative, and, in many cases, a recognizable title that carries marketing value before a single frame is shot. From a rights perspective, acquiring the right to adapt a novel means negotiating with the copyright owner, which might seem obvious to be the author. However, in some cases, the author has assigned certain subsidiary rights to the publisher in the publishing contract, or the work was created under a work-for-hire arrangement, or perhaps the rights were previously optioned or encumbered.

The agreement that governs the adaptation of a novel is most commonly an option-purchase agreement, under which the producer acquires the exclusive right to purchase the adaptation rights at a fixed or formulaic price within a specified window of time. The mechanics of that agreement will be discussed in detail later. For now, the essential point is that no producer can lawfully develop, finance, or distribute a film based on a copyrighted novel without a fully executed, properly documented agreement from the copyright owner authorizing that adaptation.

Stage Plays

Stage plays provide a particularly rich vein of source material. The dramatist, like the novelist, holds copyright in the play as a literary work. What complicates the picture is that theatrical rights and screen rights are not the same thing, and agreements governing stage productions frequently reserve, restrict, or condition the transfer of film and television rights separately. In some cases, the dramatist's agreement with a theatrical producer will include provisions that subordinate or delay the exercise of screen rights. More often, a book, film, or other project is adapted into a stage play; thus, subsidiary rights in every deal must be scrutinized and negotiated with future works in mind.

The Dramatists Guild of America, which represents playwrights, has historically taken strong positions on protecting author control over dramatists' works, and agreements negotiated under Guild standards may carry terms that a film producer finds constraining. The practical consequence is that acquiring screen rights to a stage play requires careful examination of the dramatist's existing contractual relationships, not merely a deal with the playwright herself. Clearing a stage play is rarely as simple as it appears. A due diligence review of the dramatist's underlying agreements is imperative.

News Articles and Longform Journalism

The use of a news article, magazine feature, or work of longform journalism as the basis for a film or series is more common than many writers realize, and more legally complex than most assume. A published article is a copyrighted work. The journalist who wrote it holds a copyright in her expression in the structure of the piece, the narrative choices, and the specific language even if the facts she reports are themselves unprotectable. A producer who wants to adapt a New Yorker article or a ProPublica investigation into a feature film cannot simply option the facts; she must acquire the rights to the article itself, typically through an agreement with the journalist and, depending on the publication's standard contracts, potentially with the publisher as well.

Further complicating matters is the question of life rights. Specifically, if the article's subjects are identifiable real people, their life rights may need to be separately cleared, independent of any agreement with the journalist. While the article may give you the narrative architecture and the legal predicate for development, it does not automatically authorize the portrayal of every individual named within it. Furthermore, journalism is generally given more leniency by courts when it comes to public interest topics such as right of privacy issues.

Memoir and Nonfiction Books

Nonfiction books, specifically memoir, warrant treatment separate from the novel because, while they are equally subject to copyright protection as literary works, they introduce an additional layer of rights analysis in that the subjects are real people and the events depicted actually occurred. Acquiring the right to adapt a memoir means entering into an agreement with the author or publisher, who holds the copyright in the book. But the author of a memoir must tread carefully when it comes to portraying third parties who appear in the narrative.

Other real individuals whose lives intersect with the memoir's story may have separate claims, depending on the clearance process for the published book, particularly if the proposed adaptation departs from the published text or includes material not contained in the book. The production of a memoir-based film therefore frequently requires both a literary rights agreement with the author and one or more separate life rights agreements with other subjects. We will address the specific mechanics and legal considerations of life rights agreements in Chapter 11.

Podcasts

The podcast has emerged as one of the most active sources of adaptation material in contemporary development, and the rights landscape surrounding it is still, in some respects, being worked out by the industry. A podcast, like any other original creative work, is protected by copyright from the moment of fixation, in this case, from the moment the audio is recorded. The copyright owner is typically the creator or production company behind the show, though the analysis can become complicated when the podcast is produced under a network deal, when multiple creators share ownership, or when the podcast is itself based on licensed underlying material. A true-crime podcast that investigates a real case, for example, may be based on journalistic reporting, court records, and interviews, none of which the podcast producer necessarily owns.

Acquiring the rights to adapt that podcast into a television series requires not only a deal with the podcast's copyright owner, but a careful accounting of what underlying rights that owner actually holds and what gaps remain. The podcast deal is increasingly a standard transaction in development, but it is not always a clean one. Producers who acquire podcast rights without conducting thorough underlying rights diligence do so at their own peril.

Video Games

Video game adaptations have become among the most commercially significant projects in both film and television, and they raise rights considerations that are genuinely distinctive. A video game is a composite work, meaning it encompasses audiovisual elements, musical compositions, literary elements (dialogue, narrative, world-building), software code, and often separately licensed intellectual property such as character designs or musical scores. The copyright in the game as a whole is typically owned by the game publisher, but that copyright may coexist with underlying rights held by the developer, individual contributors, or third-party licensors.

Acquiring the right to adapt a video game requires a deal with the publisher and, depending on the game's ownership structure, potentially additional clearances from developers or other rights holders. It also raises questions about which elements of the game, such as story, characters, setting, and tone, are being licensed. Also important is whether the license extends to sequels, expansions, and downloadable content that may have been released after the original title. Game adaptation agreements are among the more complex rights transactions in the industry and should be reviewed by experienced counsel.

The True Story and Life Rights

When a project is based on real events and real people rather than a preexisting creative work, the rights analysis shifts from copyright to a distinct but related category: life rights. A true story, in the strict legal sense, is not copyrightable. Facts belong to no one. But the portrayal of real, identifiable individuals in a dramatic work implicates rights of publicity, rights of privacy, and potential defamation exposure, all of which are governed by a patchwork of state law rather than federal statute.

A life rights agreement is a contract with a real person or, if that person is deceased, with their estate, in which the subject grants the producer the right to depict their life, story, and likeness in a production. Life rights deals do not eliminate all legal exposure, but they substantially reduce it and, critically, they provide the producer with the subject's cooperation and access to unpublished materials, personal recollections, and proprietary information that can be essential to a compelling and defensible production. Life rights agreements are addressed in detail in Chapter 11.

Public Domain Material

Not all source material requires a rights agreement. Works in the public domain, which is generally, works whose copyright has expired (in 2026, it would be works published before 1928), or works dedicated to the public domain by their owners may be adapted freely without authorization or payment. Shakespeare is fair game as are novels of Jane Austen. The original Dracula and Frankenstein have generated countless adaptations without a cent owed to Bram Stoker's or Mary Shelley's estates. The caveat, however, is that while the underlying public domain work is free to use, any derivative version of that work may itself be protected. A 1994 film adaptation of a nineteenth-century novel is a copyrighted work. You can adapt the novel; you cannot copy the film.

The line between inspiration and infringement becomes particularly blurry when a project draws on a public domain source but resembles a well-known existing adaptation more closely than it resembles the original. Another blurred line occurs with a book or film made internationally that may have a different copyright expiration date than that in the United States. You can see that public domain is a genuine safe harbor, but navigating it still requires attention.

Songs, Comic Books, Board Games, and Beyond

The foregoing categories represent the most common forms of source material in development, but they are not exhaustive. Musical compositions and sound recordings have served as the basis for biographical films and narrative features with each carrying its own rights clearance requirements, including synchronization licenses, master use licenses, and, in biographical contexts, life rights.

Comic books and graphic novels are now among some of the most commercially significant sources of entertainment IP, with rights typically held by publishers rather than individual artists or writers, and with adaptation agreements that frequently include extensive approval rights, sequel and franchise provisions, and complex backend structures. Board games and toys have been licensed for surprisingly large-scale productions. Who can forget the success of the Barbie movie?

Academic works, court transcripts, and government documents, which may be in the public domain or subject to fair use, have all served as the foundation for dramatic works. Even social media posts and viral internet phenomena have been optioned. The industry's appetite for recognizable IP is essentially limitless.

In every case, the analysis is the same: identify who created the underlying work, determine who currently owns the relevant rights, assess what prior encumbrances or restrictions apply, and structure an agreement that clearly and completely authorizes the intended use. The specific forms those agreements take, i.e. options, purchases, licenses, assignments, life rights deals, and the deal points that govern them are the subject of the chapters that follow. But no agreement can be intelligently negotiated without first understanding what rights are on the table.

PRO TIP:

Merely citing or crediting a source for the use of their work in your book or other work is irrelevant when it comes to copyright infringement. Instead, a fair use analysis is required.

Fair Use Considerations

When it comes to copyright law, fair use is the most frequently relied upon by creators and the least accurately understood legal theory when it comes to IP. Fair use is cited as a defense against infringement claims in contexts where it does not apply and often dismissed as irrelevant in contexts where it might genuinely matter.

Fair use is a doctrine codified in the United States at 17 U.S.C. § 107 that permits the use of copyrighted material without authorization from the copyright owner in certain circumstances. It exists because copyright law, if applied with absolute rigidity, would strangle the very creative and intellectual discourse it is meant to foster. Fair use carves out protected space for the following activities: commentary, criticism, parody, scholarship, news reporting, and transformative artistic expression. Each depends on the ability to reference, quote, and build upon existing works. However, the fair use carve-outs do not provide a blanket exemption for any use that the user subjectively believes is reasonable, proportionate, or justified.

The foundational misunderstanding takes several forms. The most common is the belief that using a small or specific quantity of copyrighted material, for example, a few lines, a brief excerpt, or a short clip, automatically qualifies as fair use. It does not. There is no numerical threshold, no word count, no percentage of the original work, that functions as a legal safe harbor. Courts have found infringement in the copying of a single sentence. They have also found fair use in the reproduction of an entire work, where the circumstances warranted it. The amount copied is one factor in the analysis, not a dispositive one. Anyone who tells you that copying fewer than a certain number of words is automatically safe is either mistaken or being deliberately imprecise.

A second common error is the belief that using material *not* for profit or not for a paying audience insulates a use from infringement liability. It does not, although it may weigh in the user's favor. A third error, particularly prevalent in the digital era, is the assumption that acknowledging the source of copied material somehow cures the infringement. Giving credit is good practice, but it is not a substitute for authorization, and it does not transform an infringing use into a permissible one.

The Four-Factor Analysis

Before setting forth the analysis used by courts in determining fair use, it's important to remember that fair use is *a defense*. That means, there is already an alleged copyright infringement in play. Therefore, if you are relying on fair use, then you are playing defense, not offense.

Section 107 of the Copyright Act sets out four factors that courts must consider in evaluating whether a particular use qualifies as fair use. These factors are not a checklist, and satisfying any one of them does not guarantee a favorable result. They are weighed together, in light of the totality of the circumstances, with no single factor controlling the outcome.

Factor 1: *The Purpose and Character of the Use*. This is generally considered the most important factor in contemporary fair use analysis, and it centers on a question the Supreme Court articulated in *Campbell v. Acuff-Rose Music* (1994): Does the new work merely supersede the original, or does it add something new, such as a different purpose, a different character, a new expression, meaning, or message? In other words, the more *transformative* the use, the more strongly this factor weighs in favor of fair use. A use that is primarily commercial in nature will face greater scrutiny but is not automatically disqualifying. Most professional creative expression would be considered commercial in some sense. What courts are really asking is whether the use serves a different function than the original, for example, in the form of criticism, commentary, or parody, or whether it simply reproduces the original for the same purpose the original was intended to serve.

Factor 2: *The Nature of the Copyrighted Work*. This factor asks what kind of work is being copied. Copyright protection is strongest for highly creative, expressive works, such as literary fiction, poetry, and music, and somewhat weaker for factual, informational, or functional works. Copying from a published work is generally treated with more leniency than copying from an unpublished one; the author's right to control the first public appearance of her work carries significant weight. In practice, this factor tends to be the least determinative of the four. The nature of the original matters, but it rarely changes the outcome of a fair use analysis by itself.

Factor 3: ***The Amount and Substantiality of the Portion Used*.** This is the factor that most commonly gets used and also misapplied in practice. Courts look at both the quantitative and qualitative dimensions of what was copied. Quantitatively, copying less is generally better but there is no magic number below which copying is automatically safe. Qualitatively, courts ask whether the portion taken represents the "heart" of the original work. Copying a few lines may constitute infringement if those lines are the most memorable, distinctive, or commercially significant part of the original. Conversely, reproducing a larger portion of a factual or functional work may be permissible if the portion taken is not qualitatively central to the work's value. The question is not simply how much was taken, but what was taken and why.

Generally speaking, it is this factor that writers often rely on without realizing it when quoting another work or using a famous quote by another author or other copyrighted source. Using a literary quote is generally regarded as fair use. Think Carl Jung, Anaïs Nin, Mark Twain. Furthermore, many well-known quotes fall within the public domain due to the age of the copyrighted source.

Factor 4: ***The Effect of the Use on the Potential Market for the Original*.** This factor is often described as the most economically significant, and in many cases carries the most weight. Courts ask whether the challenged use harms or is likely to harm the market for the original work or for licensed derivatives of it. If the new work substitutes for the original in the marketplace or if consumers would buy or access the new work instead of purchasing the original, then that substitution effect weighs heavily against fair use. Equally important is the effect on the market for licensed adaptations. If the copyright owner could reasonably license this type of use, and the user has circumvented that market by proceeding without authorization, courts will factor that into the analysis. A use that harms neither the original market nor the licensing market for the work is in much stronger fair use territory.

The Absence of Bright Lines

As mentioned previously, the four-factor test does not produce predictable, consistent outcomes. Fair use litigation is among the most fact-specific and outcome-uncertain in all of intellectual property law. Two cases with superficially similar facts can yield opposite results depending on the court, the circuit, the judge, and the particular emphasis given to each factor in the weighing process. The Second Circuit (which covers New York) and the Ninth Circuit (which covers California), which are the two federal circuits most relevant to the entertainment industry, have not always applied the factors in identical ways, and the Supreme Court has revisited the doctrine periodically without resolving all of the tensions in the lower courts' approaches.

The practical consequence means that if you are sued for infringement, you may have an argument that your use was permissible with no guarantee of success. Experienced entertainment attorneys are appropriately cautious about advising clients to proceed in reliance on fair use in commercial contexts, precisely because the doctrine's application is so fact-dependent and the cost of being wrong is so high. When in doubt, the correct course of action is to seek the advice of an attorney, not to assume your use qualifies as a defense.

When Fair Use Arises for Writers and Creators

Notwithstanding the foregoing cautions, fair use is a real and viable doctrine in the right circumstances. The following examples illustrate the kinds of situations in which a fair use argument is most commonly used with success in the context of entertainment and creative work.

Parody and Satire

The Supreme Court's decision in *Campbell v. Acuff-Rose Music* established that parody, which is a work that comments on or criticizes the original by imitating it, is among the most strongly protected forms of fair use. A film that lampoons a well-known franchise by reproducing elements of that franchise to mock or critique it is in relatively strong fair use territory. *Saturday Night Live* is a good example. However, note this important distinction: parody targets the original work itself; satire uses the original as a vehicle to comment on something else. Courts have been somewhat less sympathetic to pure satire, reasoning that a satirist, unlike a parodist, has less need to conjure the original specifically.

Criticism and Documentary Filmmaking

Documentary filmmakers regularly invoke fair use when incorporating brief clips, photographs, archival footage, or song excerpts into nonfiction works. A documentary about the history of a musical genre may need to reproduce short passages of protected songs. A biographical film may need to include news footage or photographs to establish historical context. In these contexts, the transformative purpose in the form of criticism, commentary, historical documentation combined with limited reproduction and minimal market substitution, often supports a fair use conclusion. That said, documentary producers routinely conduct errors-and-omissions insurance reviews, and insurers apply their own analysis to fair use claims. A use that feels defensible may nonetheless be excluded from coverage, creating practical complications even where the legal argument is reasonably strong.

The Rogers Test and Documentary Practice

One additional doctrine that arises in fair use, particularly in documentary filmmaking is what's known as *The Rogers Test* that originated in the Second Circuit's 1989 decision and subsequently adopted or adapted by courts across multiple jurisdictions. The case addressed a distinct but related question: when does the use of a third party's name, likeness, or trademark in an expressive work constitute actionable infringement of that party's rights of publicity? For documentary filmmakers, who routinely incorporate the names and identities of real people, commercial brands, and trademarked properties into their work, understanding how the Rogers framework applies is important.

Under the Rogers test, content that uses a third party's name or mark in an expressive work is not actionable under the Lanham Act unless the use has *no artistic relevance* to the underlying work, or if it does have some artistic relevance, then the use *explicitly misleads* consumers as to the source or content of the work. The threshold for artistic relevance is intentionally low, so then the burden shifts to whether the use is explicitly misleading, wherein the work affirmatively represents a false connection, endorsement, or sponsorship that the audience would reasonably take as genuine.

The practical application for documentary filmmakers is significant. A documentary that names a living person in its title, references a commercial product depicted in archival footage, or incorporates a trademarked logo visible in a filmed environment is not, by operation of the Rogers test, automatically exposed to right-of-publicity or Lanham Act liability provided the expressive use is genuinely connected to the documentary's subject matter and does not falsely suggest an official relationship with the mark or the person.

What the Rogers test does not do, however, is insulate a filmmaker from state-law right-of-publicity claims in jurisdictions that have declined to adopt the Rogers framework, nor does it operate as a substitute for the four-factor fair use analysis when the claim at issue is copyright infringement rather than trademark or publicity rights. These are legally distinct frameworks governing distinct causes of action. It's best not to rely on any single doctrine for clearance and yet it's important to be aware of the potential legal issues in pre- and post-production before the film moves into the distribution phase.

Incidental Use in Visual Media

When a protected work appears incidentally in a film or television production, for example, a painting visible on a wall, a billboard in the background of a scene, a news clip playing on a background TV, a fair use argument may be available. The key variables are whether the protected work is recognizable, how prominently it features in the scene, and whether its appearance serves a narrative purpose that goes beyond mere reproduction. If the protected IP is so prominent in the scene that it could *create confusion* of a sponsorship or endorsement, then the fair use line has been crossed. For shots that linger too long on brands or other protected IP, it's advisable to edit in post-production. For productions with significant budgets and distribution ambitions, it's typical to clear these uses rather than rely on a fair use because the cost of clearance is generally lower than the cost of defending the position if challenged.

Quoting from Copyrighted Works in Screenplays

A screenplay that incorporates a brief quotation from a poem, song lyric, or novel to characterize a protagonist, set a scene, or serve a dramatic purpose is invoking fair use whether the writer knows it or not. This is one of the most common and least examined fair use situations in development. The transformative nature of the use (a dramatic context rather than a competitive one), the brevity of the quotation, and the absence of market substitution often support a fair use conclusion. However, song lyrics are aggressively licensed and protected by publishers who have historically been less receptive to fair use arguments than courts in other contexts. If a script depends meaningfully on a specific copyrighted lyric or passage, then securing a license is the prudent course. The music publisher of the song generally holds the right to the lyrics and have a process by which to license the song or lyric.

Adapting Factual Events and Court Records

As noted in the previous section, facts are not copyrightable. Public court records, government documents, and reported news are generally available as source material without triggering copyright liability, though they may raise other legal concerns, such as defamation, right of publicity, and privacy rights, that require separate analysis. A screenwriter who bases a script on a court transcript, a congressional hearing, or a publicly filed document is not making a fair use argument because the documents were never protected by copyright in the first place. However, the fair use doctrine becomes relevant when the protected expression from those sources, such as the specific language of a journalist's account, rather than the underlying facts the journalist reported.

Clearance for E&O Insurance

Understanding fair use and the Rogers test is necessary, but sometimes a second layer of clearance is required, particularly for documentary filmmakers, in terms of insurance coverage for the film. No serious distributor, broadcaster, or streaming platform will accept delivery of a documentary without errors and omissions (E&O) insurance. E&O is a professional liability policy that covers the production against claims arising from the content of the film itself, including claims of copyright infringement, defamation, invasion of privacy, right-of-publicity violations, and related torts.

The insurer assesses whether the production presents an acceptable risk of being sued for infringement, and on what terms it is willing to assume that risk. E&O underwriters conduct their own clearance review as a condition of issuing a policy. The review typically encompasses the film's title; all music used, whether as source, score, or background; all archival footage, photographs, and third-party audiovisual materials incorporated into the film; the identities of all real persons depicted; any trademarks, logos, or branded materials visible in the film; and all underlying rights documentation, including any option or acquisition agreements for source material.

The production is usually required to submit a clearance report prepared by a qualified clearance professional or entertainment attorney certifying that each of these elements has been reviewed and that the production holds the rights, clearances, or a documented legal basis for every use. It is here that the fair use opinion letter becomes essential. When a production has made a decision to rely on fair use for a particular use rather than obtaining a license, the E&O underwriter will typically require, as a condition of insuring that use, a written opinion from a qualified entertainment attorney analyzing the specific use under the four-factor statutory framework and concluding, with reasoned explanation, that the use constitutes fair use as a matter of law.

A credible fair use opinion letter is a substantive legal memorandum that identifies the copyrighted work at issue, characterizes the nature and extent of the use, applies each of the four statutory factors to the specific facts, addresses any counterarguments that a rights holder might reasonably raise, and arrives at a reasoned conclusion. The letter does not guarantee that the use is fair use, but it demonstrates that the production exercised professional due diligence, which is precisely what the insurer needs to assess and price its risk.

It's important to know that not every fair use opinion letter will satisfy every underwriter. E&O insurers have their own risk tolerances. Filmmakers who have committed to a particular use on the assumption that a fair use letter will clear it for insurance purposes should confirm that assumption with their E&O broker before the film is cut. Second, the cost of obtaining a fair use opinion from a qualified entertainment attorney is a cost that should be budgeted as a production expense, not treated as an afterthought during post-production clearance. Finally, a fair use letter is not a substitute for a license when a license is obtainable. If the rights holder is identifiable, willing to negotiate, and asking for a fee that is commercially reasonable relative to the value of the use, obtaining the license is often the more prudent course.

Script Clearance

It is worth distinguishing the film clearance described above from script clearance, which is a separate and earlier exercise. Film clearance is the post-production review that supports E&O coverage and confirms that every element appearing on screen, including music, footage, trademarks, and depictions of real persons, is properly cleared. Script clearance, by contrast, is conducted on the screenplay itself, typically before principal photography begins and often during pre-production once the shooting script is locked.

A script clearance is usually performed by a professional clearance company that reads the script line by line and flags potential legal issues such as the use of real names, real businesses, trademarks, song titles and lyrics, fictional phone numbers and license plates, depictions of identifiable real persons, and any references that could give rise to defamation, right-of-publicity, or infringement claims. The clearance company then produces a script clearance report identifying each flagged item and recommending whether it should be changed, replaced with a cleared alternative, or licensed. Addressing those items at the script stage is materially less expensive than discovering them after the film has been shot, and a completed script clearance report is one of the documents the E&O underwriter will expect to see as part of the later film clearance package.

CHAPTER 4

WHAT IS CHAIN OF TITLE

You now understand that copyright exists automatically in any original work of authorship fixed in a tangible medium. You understand that copyright is not a single right but a bundle and that each component of that bundle can be transferred, licensed, retained, or encumbered independently. You understand that source material comes in many forms, that each form presents its own rights clearance challenges, and that no one may lawfully adapt a copyrighted work without authorization from the person or entity that owns the relevant rights. You understand that fair use is a defense of limited and uncertain application, not a license or a substitute for a properly negotiated agreement. All of that knowledge now converges in a single concept: *chain of title*.

Chain of title is the documented legal history of a copyright made up of a sequential record of how the ownership of a work, or the rights to exploit it, has passed from one party to another from the moment of creation to the present day. The term is borrowed from real property law, where a chain of title is the recorded history of ownership of a piece of land. Just as a lender financing the purchase of real property needs to confirm that the seller actually owns what she is purporting to sell and that no prior claims, liens, or encumbrances cloud that ownership so is the case for a studio, financier, or distributor investing in a film or television project. They too need to confirm that the producer actually owns and controls the rights she is purporting to exploit. Without that confirmation, the investment is not secure. The project cannot be insured. And in the event of a dispute, there may be no legally defensible basis for the production to exist at all.

Why Producers and Studios Require Clean Title

The practical stakes of chain of title are high enough that no sophisticated buyer, financier, or distributor will close a transaction without a title review, typically conducted by an entertainment attorney, confirming that the chain of title to the underlying material is complete, unencumbered, and legally sufficient to support the rights being conveyed. Errors-and-omissions insurers, whose policies are required by virtually every distributor before a film can be commercially released, impose the same requirement. A project that cannot demonstrate clean chain of title cannot be insured. A project that cannot be insured cannot be distributed. That can also include some film festival submissions that require films to be insured prior to screening.

PRO TIP:

For independent filmmakers who self-distribute, i.e. YouTube or other online platforms, you will not be required to have your film insured, however, you take on the risk as if you were the distributor—because you are the distributor.

If copyright is a bundle of rights, and if each component of that bundle can be separately transferred or encumbered, then the only way to confirm that a producer actually holds a clean, unencumbered right to produce, distribute, and exploit a film based on a particular piece of source material is to trace every link in the chain from the original author to the present moment. A single broken link, i.e. an unexecuted agreement, an ambiguously worded assignment, an option that expired before it was exercised, an underlying rights deal that was never properly documented, can cloud the title, rendering the entire project legally vulnerable.

What Clean Chain of Title Looks Like

Think of a clean chain of title as a straight, unbroken line from the original copyright owner to the party currently seeking to exploit the work. What that line looks like in practice depends on the nature of the source material and the history of the project. For an original screenplay with a single author and no underlying rights, the chain may be short consisting of the writer's copyright registration, a properly executed assignment or work-for-hire agreement conveying rights to the producer or studio, and any subsequent agreements governing the writer's services or separated rights. That is relatively clean. For screenwriters who produce their own projects, you can see how much simpler chain of title is.

Imagine a film based on a published novel that was adapted from a magazine article, featuring a real historical figure whose estate holds life rights, with a screenplay written by three successive writers under separate guild agreements. For a project with such complex rights, the chain of title documentation may include dozens of agreements. Each link in that chain must be present, properly executed, and legally sufficient. The record typically includes: copyright registrations for the underlying work and the screenplay; all option agreements and their extensions; the purchase or assignment agreement that conveyed the underlying rights; any work-for-hire or certificate of authorship agreements executed by contributing writers; guild agreements governing separated rights or writing credit; any life rights agreements with real-person subjects.

The key word throughout is *executed.* An agreement that was negotiated but never signed does not exist for chain of title purposes.

A handshake deal, an exchange of emails, or a term sheet that was never papered into a formal agreement do not constitute a link in the chain. You can see the importance of having legal counsel to create a valid legal chain of title from the beginning.

Copyright assignments must be in writing and signed by the party conveying the rights under 17 U.S.C. § 204(a). An oral agreement to assign a copyright is legally unenforceable, regardless of what the parties understood or intended. This requirement catches more projects than one might expect. In the early stages of development, when relationships are friendly and trust is high, it is tempting to proceed informally, but the consequences of that informality can come back around in adverse ways.

Common Defects That Cloud the Title

A *cloud on the title* is any defect, ambiguity, or unresolved claim that calls into question whether the producer holds the rights she purports to hold. Clouds arise in predictable patterns, and understanding those patterns is the first step toward avoiding them. The following include the most common defects encountered in entertainment chain of title reviews.

Unsigned or incomplete agreements

The most basic defect is an agreement that was drafted and negotiated but never fully executed by all required parties. A partially signed agreement is not an agreement for chain of title purposes. The fix is to obtain the missing signature(s) but it requires locating parties who may have moved, changed representation, or lost interest in the project. The longer a project sits in development without properly executed paperwork, the more difficult this becomes.

Expired options that were never exercised or renewed

An option agreement grants the producer the right to purchase underlying rights within a defined period. If the producer fails to exercise the option before it expires or fails to renew it on the terms provided in the agreement, then the option lapses and the rights revert to the owner. A project that has been in development for years may be resting on an option chain in which one or more options have silently expired. The producer may not know this, and the underlying rights owner may not have flagged it. However, the title reviewer will find it and the production will halt until it is resolved.

Ambiguous or overbroad assignments

An assignment that purports to convey rights in vague or undefined terms, for example, "all rights in and to the Work," without specifying the territory, medium, or duration, may be legally sufficient in some respects while leaving material ambiguities that a sophisticated buyer or insurer may flag. Similarly, an assignment that attempts to convey rights the assignor did not possess, or rights that were already encumbered under a prior agreement, is defective to that extent. You cannot convey more rights than you own, and an assignment of overreaching scope does not cure the underlying deficiency.

Unresolved co-authorship claims

When a work has multiple authors, then each contributing author may hold an ownership interest in the work. This includes scripts that may have passed through several drafts under different writers without a written agreement in place. As discussed earlier, a joint work is one prepared by two or more authors with the intention that their contributions be merged into inseparable or interdependent parts of a unitary whole. Each co-author of a joint work has the right to exploit the work independently, subject to a duty to account to the other co-authors. A studio acquiring a screenplay that is arguably a joint work must obtain conveyances from all co-authors, or else risk a subsequent claim from a contributing writer whose interest was not properly addressed.

Underlying rights that were never cleared

As discussed in the source material section, a screenplay based on a novel, article, podcast, or other protected work requires a properly documented agreement with the underlying rights owner. A project in which the writer adapted source material without authorization, or in which an early producer assumed rights were cleared when they were not, has a potentially fatal defect at the base of the chain. Discovering that a project's underlying rights were never properly cleared after years of development and significant expenditure is among the worst-case-scenario outcomes in the business.

Missing certificates of authorship

When a producer engages a writer on a work-for-hire basis, the agreement should include a Certificate of Authorship (COA). A COA is a short, standalone document in which the writer confirms that the work was created as a work made for hire, assigns all rights in the event the work-for-hire characterization does not hold up, and warrants that the work is original and does not infringe any third-party rights. These certificates are routine instruments, but they are frequently omitted in deals made early in a project's development when the parties are moving quickly and the paperwork feels like a mere formality.

What to Do When There Is a Cloud on the Title

Discovering a cloud on the title during a deal does not necessarily mean the project is dead. It means the defect must be identified, disclosed, and remediated before the transaction can close. The approach depends on the nature and severity of the cloud.

The first step is always accurate diagnosis. Not every defect is equally serious. An unsigned amendment to a secondary agreement is a different order of problem from an entirely unexecuted underlying rights deal. A title opinion that identifies a cloud should specify its nature, its likely legal consequence if unaddressed, and the range of remediation options available. The attorney's job at this stage is not to minimize the problem but to characterize it accurately so that the parties can make informed decisions about how to proceed.

Where a defect arises from a missing or incomplete agreement, the straightforward remedy is what's known as a *nunc pro tunc* execution where an agreement is executed in the present but reflects the original execution date. Courts generally recognize nunc pro tunc agreements as effective to cure defective or missing instruments, provided both parties are willing to execute and provided no intervening rights have attached in the interim. Obtaining a nunc pro tunc agreement requires locating the relevant party, negotiating the terms of the cure, and ensuring the instrument is properly documented. It can be time-consuming, and it is not always possible when the original party is deceased, dissolved, or uncooperative. But where it is available, it is usually the cleanest and most efficient resolution.

When the cloud arises from a potential competing claim, such as a co-author who was not part of the original conveyance, a prior option holder who may argue the option was improperly terminated, or a party who believes they contributed authorship to the work, the remedy is in the form of a quitclaim or assignment agreement. This is a document in which the claimant relinquishes any claim they may have to the relevant rights, whether or not they formally acknowledge that such a claim exists. Quitclaims are intentionally drafted in broad, catch-all language precisely because their purpose is to neutralize ambiguity rather than resolve a definitive legal dispute. They are among the most practically useful instruments in chain of title work and obtaining them proactively from any party who might plausibly assert a claim is a standard method of curing the title.

In situations where the underlying rights were never properly cleared or where the source material was used without authorization, the only remedy is to go back to the beginning and negotiate the agreement that should have been negotiated before development began. That conversation is almost always more expensive and more difficult than it would have been at the outset. The underlying rights owner is now aware of the project's existence and progress and is therefore in a materially stronger negotiating position than they would have been before any development expenditure was made. This is one of the most important reasons to address chain of title at the earliest possible stage of any project.

Chain of Title as a Creative Discipline

Writers sometimes experience chain of title as an administrative burden that belongs to producers, business affairs executives, and entertainment attorneys rather than to the people doing the actual creative work. However, the chain of title is the necessary infrastructure that makes creative work commercially viable. Regardless of its creative merit, a screenplay without clean title is, for practical purposes, unsellable because the legal foundation necessary to build a production on top of it has not been properly constructed.

Understanding chain of title gives a writer the ability to protect their own work before problems arise. The writer who registers her copyright, executes clean agreements with every collaborator, clears underlying rights before development begins, and insists on proper documentation at every stage of a project's evolution is practicing the discipline it takes to sustain a career as a professional writer or creator.

ACT II

Enter the Dealmaker

Daniel had been writing for seven years when a producer he met at a festival expressed genuine interest in his pilot. The producer was credible and at a mid-tier cable network. When the producer's assistant emailed a shopping agreement and said, casually, "just the standard stuff, sign whenever," Daniel read it quickly, noticed it was only four pages, concluded that four pages could not contain that many traps, and signed.

The agreement gave the producer an eighteen-month shopping period with two renewal options, each exercisable unilaterally. It granted shopping rights not just to the pilot but to any derivative works, sequels, or spin-offs "based on or inspired by" the underlying material. It included no reversion provision. It contained a broad warranty clause that Daniel did not read carefully and could not have interpreted without legal training. And it was governed by the law of a state where Daniel did not live and had never conducted business.

When the producer went quiet after month three, Daniel had no practical mechanism for getting his project back. When a second producer expressed interest in the same material fourteen months later, Daniel had nothing to offer. The agreement he had signed was still in effect.

CHAPTER 5

YOUR ROLE AS THE DEALMAKER

The skills that make you an exceptional writer are likely not the qualities that will protect your intellectual property, secure your backend participation, or ensure that you retain the right to reacquire your material if a producer goes dark for two years. These skillsets require wearing different hats.

This chapter is about taking on a different POV than you may be used to and learning to see your project not as your creative child but as a property with quantifiable value, identifiable risks, and negotiable terms. You may write the most brilliant script of the decade, but if you sign the wrong agreement, you may find yourself legally prohibited from ever writing the sequel, stripped of your right to credit, or paid a fraction of what your work ultimately generates. Even worse, the script may end up in a drawer never seeing the light of day again.

The Dual Role Problem

Most writers enter negotiations in a disadvantaged position because they are being asked to perform two roles simultaneously: the role of the writer or creator of the project, whose instinct is to protect the work and get it made, and the role of the dealmaker, whose function is to protect the writer and get fair terms. These roles are in inherent tension with one another.

The writer wants the deal to close. The tendency can be to worry that asking for too much will cause the producer to walk. Perhaps you are emotionally invested and therefore susceptible to flattery, to urgency, and to the seductive promise that once the project gets made, everything else will work itself out.

The dealmaker, by contrast, understands that the agreement executed before production begins is the document that will govern the relationship for years, sometimes decades, to come. The dealmaker is not indifferent to whether the project gets made; the dealmaker simply understands that a bad deal is often worse than no deal at all. The goal in reading this book is to develop and internalize the dealmaker's perspective without abandoning what makes you a writer.

It's important to note that in a negotiation, the other party—whether a producer, a studio, a financier, or a distribution company—is not your collaborator. They may be entirely well-intentioned. But in the moment of negotiating terms, they have interests that diverge from yours. They want to pay less; you want to receive more. They want broader rights; you want to retain more control. They want fewer obligations; you want more protections.

None of this makes them a villain, it simply makes each of you counterparties. And the good news is that both parties want the project to move forward. That's what you have in common and that's also the common denominator that will likely bring both parties to an agreeable outcome when it comes to negotiating an agreement. The chapters that follow will give you the vocabulary, the frameworks, and the practical tools to negotiate effectively.

PRO TIP:

Every agreement is initially drafted in favor of the party drafting it. It is up to the other party to tilt the scales more evenly, if not more in their favor.

General Negotiation Tips

There is an entire area of study devoted to the art and science of negotiation, called game theory, built around concepts like BATNA, anchoring, and the zone of possible agreement. This section is not going to attempt to replicate those theories, but it will give you a working set of principles that are directly applicable to the entertainment industry, grounded in the practical realities of how deals actually get made in this business.

Let Someone Else Do the Talking

First thing to know about negotiating in the industry is that whenever economically feasible, hire an entertainment attorney, not a general practice attorney, not your cousin who passed the bar, but a working entertainment attorney with transactional experience in film and television. Not just to "look it over," but to actually negotiate on your behalf.

It's understandable to want to save money and DIY it. However, it will likely cost you more money down the road. Consider how real estate transactions work. When a buyer and a seller are both represented by agents, neither party communicates directly with the other about price, terms, or counteroffers. The agents do that. It benefits both parties by creating distance, slowing things down in productive ways, filtering out emotional reactivity, and allowing each party's representative to take positions that the principal might not otherwise take themselves. The buyer's agent can say "my client won't go above four-fifty" without the buyer having to watch the seller's face fall and feel the social pressure to immediately soften the position. The seller's agent can counter at four-seventy-five without the seller feeling as though they are being greedy or difficult. The principals stay out of it, the agents manage the negotiation, and both sides typically end up with a cleaner result than they would have achieved negotiating it themselves.

The same dynamic applies in entertainment transactions. When your attorney makes a demand or holds a position, it's professional. When you make the same demand or hold the same position, it is personal. Producers, studios, and their representatives negotiate deals every day. They are experienced and almost always prefer to work with a professional on the other side.

Your attorney also provides a mechanism that is extraordinarily useful in any negotiation. I call it playing the "bad cop." For example, "My attorney won't let me sign this without …." is a great tactic in entertainment dealmaking. It removes you from the confrontation entirely. You are not being difficult. Your attorney is being difficult. This separation of the business relationship from the personal relationship is a structural advantage that professional representation provides, and it has real, quantifiable value over the life of a deal.

There is a cost-benefit calculation here that writers tend to get wrong. An entertainment attorney's fees on a standard option-purchase negotiation are not trivial, but they are modest in comparison to what is actually at stake. A writer who saves two thousand dollars in legal fees by negotiating their own deal and in doing so fails to secure a meaningful reversion clause, accepts a broader rights grant than necessary, or misses a backend provision that would have entitled them to a percentage of net profits has made a bad deal. That's not to mention the money left on the table by not procuring a higher price on the option and/or purchase payment.

Seeing Your Project Objectively

One of the most practically useful skills in any negotiation is the ability to assess the value of what you are bringing to the table without inflation or false modesty. Writers tend to err in both directions. Some undervalue their material out of insecurity or eagerness, accepting terms that no reasonably informed party would accept. Others overvalue it in ways that lead to unrealistic demands and collapsed deals.

What is your script, your novel, your life story actually worth in the marketplace? The answer is: it depends. As annoying as that is, it's true, it depends on a number of factors: your professional credits and track record; the commercial viability of the genre and subject matter; whether the underlying material has been optioned or developed before; whether there is competitive interest from other producers; and the identity and resources of the party across the table. We will return to each of these variables in detail in later chapters. For now, the point is simply that value is contextual, relational, and, to a meaningful degree, negotiable.

For creatives, it's easy to conflate the artistic value of your work with its market value. These are related but distinct concepts. A script can be artistically extraordinary and commercially marginal. It can also be commercially compelling and artistically unremarkable. The market does not always reward what deserves to be rewarded.

PRO TIP:

Your job as dealmaker is to extract the best available terms for the specific project you have, in the specific market you are operating in, at this *particular moment* in time.

Know Your Leverage

In a negotiation, leverage is the set of advantages that makes the other party more willing to give you what you want. Understanding your leverage by not inflating it or underestimating it, but assessing it with clarity, is the foundational analytical task of any negotiation.

In the entertainment industry, leverage takes several recognizable forms. Professional credits are perhaps the most straightforward. A writer with a produced studio credit, a Writers Guild award, or an established track record in a particular genre is simply in a different conversation than a writer with none of those things. This is not a value judgment about the quality of the work, but a reflection of how the market prices a proven track record. In an increasingly tight market of studio acquisitions, a proven track record can make a remarkable difference. An established writer reduces the producer's perceived risk, which translates directly into negotiating power. If you have credits, know which ones matter to the person across the table and be prepared to make them relevant.

PRO TIP:

Start an IMDb account as soon as you can and record your credits to start building your profile.

Competitive interest is the second major source of leverage. If another producer, studio, or financier has expressed genuine interest in your project that's measurable leverage. The operative word is *genuine*. Fabricated competitive interest is a tactic that experienced buyers can usually detect, and when detected, it damages your credibility in ways that are difficult to repair. If you have real competitive interest, communicate it clearly and let the market work for you. If you do not, do not pretend that you do.

The commercial profile of your project itself is also a source of leverage that writers consistently undervalue. Does your script address a subject matter that is currently marketable? Is it based on underlying material, such as a published novel, a true story, a news article, that has a demonstrable audience? Is it set up as a vehicle for a specific actor or director whose attachment would create value? These factors are what producers and buyers actually use to justify acquisitions internally, and if your project has them, you should understand their value and price accordingly.

The flip side of this is that leverage you do not have cannot be manufactured through aggressive posturing. Overplaying a weak hand in an entertainment negotiation does not typically result in a better deal. It results in a slower, more adversarial deal, or no deal at all. The most effective negotiators in this industry are not the most aggressive ones, they are the ones who know exactly what their position is worth without apology and also without excess.

Anchor Early and Anchor High — But Not Absurdly

The anchoring effect is one of the most well-documented theories in negotiation psychology. Whichever party establishes the first number in a negotiation sets the cognitive reference point around which all subsequent discussion will orbit. This is true even when both parties know that the opening offer is a negotiating position rather than a genuine valuation. The anchor shapes expectations and therefore the outcomes.

In entertainment transactions, this principle suggests that you should, when possible, allow your attorney to put the first number on the table. The number should reflect the high end of what a reasonable, informed party in your position might legitimately expect, given your credits, the project's commercial profile, and the buyer's known deal history. It should not be a number you invented to see what happens. It should be a number you can defend, informed by actual market data, and set at a level that gives you room to negotiate without immediately signaling desperation by accepting a counter.

A corresponding discipline on the other side is that you should know your walk-away point before you begin. The walk-away point is the minimum set of terms below which you will not sign. It's best not determined in the heat of the negotiation, but in advance, in conversation with your attorney, with clear eyes and no emotional investment in any particular outcome. Writers who enter negotiations without a defined walk-away point almost always end up accepting terms they later regret, because in the moment, the pressure to close the deal overwhelms the judgment that would have said no.

PRO TIP:

It is customary for the producer, or buyer, to present the agreement to the creative, or talent side, since it is them making the offer. If so, the agreement will be initially drafted in the drafter's favor, and they expect it to be negotiated.

Silence as a Tool

Most people are uncomfortable with silence in a conversation, and negotiations are no exception. When an offer is made and not immediately accepted, there is a nearly universal human impulse to explain the offer, to soften it, or to add concessions that were not requested. Experienced negotiators know this and use silence deliberately. Less experienced negotiators fill it unnecessarily and, in doing so, give up ground for free.

When your attorney receives a term sheet or a counteroffer, there is no obligation to respond immediately. Take time to review, to confer, and to formulate a considered response. That's standard professional practice. If you get urgency back in the form of "we need an answer by end of week," "we have other projects we're looking at," or "the window on this is closing" know that that's more of a pressure tactic rather than a genuine deadline. Your attorney will help you distinguish between real time constraints and manufactured ones. When in doubt, take the time you need. A deal that disappears because you took three days to review it was probably not a deal you wanted.

Do Not Negotiate Against Yourself

Negotiating against yourself means making concessions that the other party did not ask for, softening positions before they have been tested, or preemptively accepting less favorable terms because you have already convinced yourself that the other side will never agree to what you actually want.

Creatives are particularly susceptible to this pattern because they have usually been living with the emotional weight of getting a project made for a long time before a deal is on the table. The prospect of losing the deal activates all of the fear and insecurity instincts discussed at the beginning of this chapter. The result is that writers frequently enter the room having already given away things that the producer would have been perfectly willing to leave on the table.

Instead, ask for what you want, and then wait to see what the other side says. If they reject it, they will tell you. If they counter, you will negotiate. But do not preemptively fold a position that has not been challenged. You do not know what the other side will accept until they tell you, and you will never find out if you have already told them no on their behalf.

Everything Is a Package

Entertainment deals almost always involve multiple deal points simultaneously and thus it's counterproductive to fight over each point in isolation. Option price, purchase price, screen credit, backend participation, reversion rights, approval rights, sequel and remake rights are not independent variables and should be negotiated as a whole.

This means that conceding on one point should be conditioned on receiving something in return on another. If a producer cannot meet your purchase price, perhaps they can offer improved backend terms, an accelerated reversion trigger, or a more favorable credit position. If a studio requires a broader rights grant than you would prefer to give, perhaps they can offer a higher option fee or a shorter initial option period. The point is that every concession you make has value, and that value should not be given away without receiving something in exchange. Your attorney will help you understand which points have real practical significance in your specific transaction and which are worth trading in exchange for gains elsewhere.

Put It in Writing

This last point is the simplest and frequently ignored. In the entertainment industry, deals are routinely discussed, agreed to in principle, and even partially executed on the basis of oral agreements, emails, and deal memos that are treated as binding by one party and as preliminary by another.

The practical rule is this that if a material term has been agreed upon, confirm it in writing in whatever form is available to you. An email saying "to confirm our conversation, the parties have agreed to the following terms" is not a contract. But it is a contemporaneous record that will matter enormously if the deal is later disputed. Do not rely on handshakes, goodwill, or the other party's assurances that the formal agreement will "reflect what we discussed." Ensure that it does.

The entertainment industry runs on relationships, but it also runs on contracts. Navigate both with professionalism to achieve the most success.

CHAPTER 6

YOUR PROFESSIONAL TEAM

While this book is not a substitute for an attorney or other representative, it is designed to make you a more informed client who understands the industry well enough to ask the right questions, identify the right concerns, and recognize when you need representation.

When to Hire an Entertainment Attorney

The short answer is you need an attorney when there is a deal on the table and in some instances before then in order to get the right deal in place. Creators often resist hiring attorneys for a handful of predictable reasons. The fee seems high relative to the deal. The agreement looks *simple*. The producer seems trustworthy. The project feels too early-stage to justify the expense. These are understandable instincts but consistently proven wrong.

PRO TIP:

Simple is rarely good. A "simple agreement" usually means it's a short agreement which translates into an agreement with missing provisions.

A competent entertainment attorney reviewing a standard option or shopping agreement will charge you somewhere between five hundred and fifteen hundred dollars for that review, depending on the complexity of the deal and the attorney's market. That fee, in the context of what you stand to lose by signing an unfavorable agreement, is small. Even if the upfront option payment is a modest sum, the rights to *your* project are at stake. That includes the right to your story, the right to write the sequel, the right to get your material back if nothing happens with it, and the right to be paid fairly if it becomes a hit.

Why You Should Rarely (if Ever) Use Online or Borrowed Agreements

It can be very tempting to download a contract template from the internet or even one you borrow from a colleague. Just fill in the blanks and call it a deal. A lot of startups in the industry do this and to be honest, many get away with it. That is, until it blows up in a way that is expensive to fix.

The first problem with an online or borrowed agreement is: *whose side was it drafted for?* Every contract is based in duality. Every clause, every defined term, every carefully placed exception is an argument made on behalf of the party whose attorney wrote it. When you pull a form off a legal website, or when a producer hands you an agreement and tells you it is "standard," you have no idea whose interests that document was originally designed to protect. You do not know whether it was drafted by a studio's in-house counsel to minimize rights reversions. You do not know whether it was written for a rights holder, a licensee, a financier, or a distributor.

The second problem is equally dangerous: *just because someone else used it and nothing went wrong does not mean it is a good agreement.* Your friend used a shopping agreement they found online, and their project got made, and everyone is happy. Good for them.

What that tells you is that no one tested the agreement. Who knows whether it would have held up if they had. Contracts are not evaluated by whether the parties are happy when things are going well. They are evaluated by what happens when something goes wrong. A producer goes silent, financing collapses, a third party makes a competing rights claim, or when someone decides the deal no longer serves their interests and looks for a way out. A defective agreement is a latent problem. It sits there, appearing perfectly functional until the moment it fails you.

The third problem is what a poorly constructed agreement can do to your chain of title. As discussed in the previous chapter, chain of title is the documentary record that establishes the unbroken sequence of rights ownership from the original creator to whoever currently holds the rights to develop, produce, and distribute the work. If you are going to attach a studio, close a financing deal, or sell your project to a distributor, that distributor's entertainment attorney is going to order a chain of title review. And if that review turns up an agreement that is ambiguous, improperly executed, missing essential representations, or otherwise defective, you may find that what you thought was a clean set of rights is, in fact, encumbered or not established at all.

A form agreement that neglects certain procedural imperatives or uses loose language can end up being a cloud on title. The same logic applies to borrowed agreements. You are inheriting every assumption that document makes about the parties, the rights, the applicable law, and the industry context in which it was drafted. Those assumptions may have no relationship to your situation whatsoever.

None of this means that every agreement you execute needs to be a hundred-page studio deal with seventeen exhibits. It means that whatever agreement you use should be drafted or reviewed by a qualified entertainment attorney who understands the specific transaction, the specific rights at issue, and the specific jurisdiction whose law will govern the deal. The cost of a properly drafted agreement is, in virtually every case, a fraction of the cost of litigating or untangling a defective one. The form you downloaded for free may end up being the most expensive document you ever signed.

The Short Agreement Problem

A producer approaches you about your screenplay. The project is a strong fit for their slate and they are enthusiastic. They send over a Shopping Agreement in the form of a single page, clean and readable, with none of the intimidating density you associate with legal documents. It looks something like this:

> *SHOPPING AGREEMENT. This agreement is entered into as of [DATE] between [WRITER] ("Owner") and [PRODUCER] ("Producer"). Owner hereby grants Producer the exclusive right to shop, pitch, and package the screenplay currently titled "[TITLE]" (the "Property") to studios, networks, and financiers for a period of twelve (12) months. In consideration of Producer's efforts, Owner agrees not to shop the Property independently or through any third party during the Term. This agreement shall be governed by the laws of the State of California. Owner acknowledges receipt of One Dollar ($1.00) and other good and valuable consideration.*

It is short, legible, and seems innocent enough. But what it leaves out is crucial. It does not define what constitutes "shopping" or what level of effort the producer is obligated to make. It does not specify what happens if the producer does nothing for twelve months; your project simply sits, exclusively encumbered, while the producer pursues other work. It contains no reversion clause meaning there is no automatic mechanism by which your rights return to you if the producer fails to attach a buyer, a financier, or a production commitment within the Term. It does not address what happens at the expiration of the Term. Can the producer extend unilaterally? Can they assert a right of first negotiation on a subsequent option? The agreement is silent as to all of those terms.

The agreement also does not address what happens if the producer's shopping efforts generate interest but no deal. Can that producer later claim an entitlement to a producer credit, an attachment fee, or a percentage of a subsequently negotiated option simply because they introduced the project to a buyer? Without a written agreement that expressly limits the producer's compensation and credits to specific, defined circumstances, you may find yourself in a dispute that, even if you ultimately prevail, costs you far more in attorney's fees than a proper agreement would have cost you at the outset.

A one-page document (or in some cases, an email) that grants exclusive rights for twelve months is a binding legal instrument that restricts what you can do with your own work, and its silence on key terms is likely not an oversight. An experienced entertainment attorney reads a short agreement and immediately begins cataloguing what is missing. Reviewing an agreement for what is absent is as important as what is present. This is one of the best examples of why the cost of counsel is almost always worth it.

Throughout the chapters that follow, we will return to examples where the question "should I hire an attorney?" has a clear answer. In virtually every case, that answer is yes. The agreements that govern your creative rights will outlast your enthusiasm for any particular project, and you want those agreements drafted by someone who is paid to think about what happens when things go wrong.

What About Using AI?

Artificial intelligence tools have become increasingly capable of producing contract language that looks, at first glance, authoritative and complete. A writer who prompts a generative AI system to draft an option agreement may receive something that resembles a professionally prepared instrument. The output may be internally coherent, grammatically fluent, and still be entirely unsuitable for the specific transaction at hand.

The truth is a legal novice doesn't know what they don't know. An AI model drafts from patterns. It doesn't know your leverage, your dealmaking history, the identity of the counterparty, what that counterparty's standard positions are, or which provisions are genuinely negotiable in the current market. It cannot tell you that the reversion clause it generated would be considered aggressive by any working business affairs executive in the industry, or that the backend definition it produced is so favorable to you that no studio will accept it without substantial revision. I've had clients present me with an AI analysis of an agreement that, while it may have some technically legitimate points, was out of context for the actual deal. In the end, it took more billable time for me to review their AI analysis than it would have without it.

That said, AI can be a useful orientation tool to familiarize yourself with unfamiliar terminology before a meeting, to generate a preliminary checklist of deal points for a particular transaction type, or to pressure-test your own understanding of a concept. For example, if you are reviewing a draft agreement and encounter a provision you do not recognize, using AI to explain the general function of that provision is a reasonable first step, but not a substitute for asking your attorney what that provision means in the context of *this* agreement, with *this* counterparty, under *these* circumstances.

The principle is the same one that governs the use of template agreements: they can be a useful starting point, but beyond that they create a false sense of security. Use AI to educate yourself, to generate questions, to build familiarity with structure and terminology, but it is ill-advised to use it as a substitute for counsel.

Managers vs. Agents vs. Attorneys

The differences between an "agent," "manager," and "attorney" deserve a discussion because they are distinct professional relationships, each governed by different regulatory frameworks, each carrying different legal obligations to the writer or artist, and each serving a different function in one's career. Conflating them or assuming that any one of them alone is sufficient is simply untrue. This section will define each role with some precision, address the fee structures that govern each relationship, and explain the role of each.

The Talent Agent

An agent is licensed to procure employment on behalf of their client. In California, which (to date) governs more entertainment transactions than any other state, talent agents are regulated under the California Talent Agencies Act (TAA), Labor Code §§ 1700 et seq., which requires anyone who "procures, offers, promises, or attempts to procure employment or engagements" for an artist to hold a talent agency license issued by the California Labor Commissioner. Agents who operate without a license are subject to having their contracts voided by the Labor Commissioner on petition by the talent they represent.

The practical consequence of this regulatory structure means that agents are the only category of representatives who are legally authorized, in California and most states, to solicit employment opportunities on a writer's behalf, pitch the writer to studios and production companies for specific assignments, and negotiate the terms of those engagements as a disclosed representative. Everything else an agent does, from reviewing agreements, advising on strategy, building relationships with buyers, flows from this core function.

Agents typically represent a writer on a commission basis. The standard commission rate for a literary agent in the entertainment industry is ten percent of the writer's gross compensation on transactions the agent procured or was a procuring cause of. That commission is typically earned on the transaction, not on receipt of funds, though the practical mechanics of collection vary. The agency agreement defines the scope of the agent's authority, the term of the relationship, and the tail, meaning the period after termination during which the agent continues to be entitled to commission on deals that were in process or resulted from the agent's efforts during the representation period.

PRO TIP:

The agent's primary role to procure employment is a function no other representative can perform on your behalf without a license and is the reason that securing agency representation remains the primary objective of most writers.

The major agencies, including WME, CAA, and UTA, represent large rosters of talent across multiple departments. An individual agent at one of these firms may carry a client list of dozens of writers. Their function is transactional and relational. They know who is buying what, they have standing relationships with the decision-makers at studios and streamers, and they can get material read and considered in rooms that would otherwise be closed. What they typically do not do is sit with a writer for two hours discussing the thematic arc of a pilot or advising on which career move best serves the writer's long-term positioning. That is the manager's territory.

Advantages of Agents: Agency representation provides access to the formal submission ecosystem and the relationships that drive the highest-value transactions. A well-placed agent at a major agency can open doors that no other representative can open. The regulatory framework provides meaningful protections for guild franchise requirements, Labor Commissioner oversight, and a defined body of law governing the relationship. The standard commission rate of ten percent is lower than the manager's fifteen percent, making the agency relationship the more cost-efficient of the two for writers generating significant transaction volume.

Disadvantages of Agents: The agent's attention is divided among a large roster of clients, and a new or mid-career writer may not command significant agent attention between transactions. The agent's incentive is to close deals, which means the agent's interest in the specific terms of any given transaction may be less intense than the writer's. Agents are not considered career developers that the writer needs for strategic guidance on long-term positioning. And for writers who cannot yet attract an agent, the entire framework is simply inaccessible until some threshold of professional recognition is achieved.

The Manager

A manager's role is, in principle, advisory and developmental rather than transactional. Managers are not licensed under the TAA and are therefore not authorized to procure employment in California. This distinction has generated significant litigation over the years, because the line between "procurement" and "guidance" is not always obvious in practice. The California Supreme Court addressed aspects of this tension in *Marathon Entertainment, Inc. v. Blasi* (2008) 42 Cal.4th 974, and the practical industry posture since then has been an uneasy equilibrium where managers routinely engage in activities that look quite a lot like procurement without holding agency licenses. This practice persists largely because many of the writers they represent either do not object or do not appreciate the legal significance of the distinction.

What managers are legally permitted to do is provide career guidance, develop the writer's body of work, facilitate introductions, package projects, and generally function as a long-term strategic partner. A manager who is actively connected in the industry will often have production company relationships that allow them to attach themselves or their company to a writer's project as a producer. This is a common arrangement that partially explains why many managers are as invested in the success of specific projects as they are in the writer's overall career trajectory.

The standard manager's commission is fifteen percent of the writer's gross compensation on represented transactions, though rates of ten percent are not uncommon with more boutique management companies, and the precise scope of what triggers the commission obligation should be addressed explicitly in the management agreement. Writers who have both an agent and a manager will typically pay a combined commission of twenty-five percent on covered transactions, which is a significant but generally accepted cost of having robust representation across both functions.

PRO TIP:

A manager with production credits and strong producing relationships can be more valuable to an unproduced writer than a mid-tier agent at a large agency because the manager can develop material, attach to the project, and create the conditions under which an agent becomes interested. For that reason, procuring a manager first and an agent second is common.

It is also worth noting that the manager's ethical and fiduciary obligations to the writer are less formally defined than that of an agent. Agents, as licensed representatives, are subject to regulation by the Labor Commissioner and by guild franchise agreements that impose specific obligations on how they may deal with their clients. Managers operate without that regulatory framework. A management agreement is a private contract, and its terms, including what happens upon termination, how disputes are resolved, and what the manager's obligations are if their interests and the writer's interests diverge, are determined entirely by what the parties negotiate and document. This makes the management agreement a document that warrants careful attorney review before it is executed, a point to which will be further discussed below.

Advantages of a Manager: A well-connected manager can provide the career development and strategic guidance that agents do not typically offer. For unproduced writers, a manager with production relationships can create the conditions under which agency representation becomes available by developing material to a level of professional polish, attaching to a project, and taking it to the market in a way that generates the kind of interest that attracts agent attention. The management relationship is also typically more personal and more invested than the agency relationship. A manager with a small roster may dedicate substantially more attention to any individual client than an agent at a major agency.

Disadvantages: The commission rate is higher, the regulatory protections are weaker, and the term is typically longer than that of agents. The absence of a licensing requirement means the quality and ethics of management services vary considerably, and the writer has fewer institutional remedies if the manager performs poorly or acts in bad faith. The producer attachment dynamic creates a structural conflict of interest that the writer must actively manage.

The Entertainment Attorney

The entertainment attorney holds a different role than either the agent or the manager, although sometimes overlapping in practical terms. An attorney's primary function is legal in the form of reviewing, negotiating, and drafting agreements; advising on rights issues, chain of title, and regulatory compliance; and representing the writer's legal interests in disputes. Attorneys are licensed by their state bars, subject to professional responsibility rules that impose duties of loyalty, confidentiality, and competence, and bound by an ethical obligation to act in the client's interests rather than their own. Those obligations are enforceable through the bar disciplinary process in a way that neither agent nor manager conduct is.

What distinguishes the entertainment attorney from the other two representatives is not merely function but access. In a market where an unproduced writer may struggle to attract a legitimate agent and may not yet have the profile to interest a well-connected manager, an entertainment attorney can be retained immediately, on a straightforward fee-for-service or transactional basis, without any threshold of industry recognition or results-based commission. The attorney does not need to believe in the writer's long-term commercial viability in order to review a contract. The attorney is paid for the service, not for the outcome.

Fee structures for entertainment attorneys vary considerably depending on the nature of the engagement. Hourly billing is the standard for transactional work, such as reviewing agreements, advising on rights, and consulting on deal structure. Rates among entertainment attorneys in major markets, such as Los Angeles and New York, primarily range from approximately $300 to $800 per hour for experienced transactional practitioners, with higher rates at larger firms and lower rates at boutique practices focused specifically on independent film and emerging writer clients. A writer retaining an attorney on an hourly basis for a straightforward option agreement review and negotiation should expect a fee in the range of $750 to $2,500, depending on the complexity of the transaction and the amount of back-and-forth the negotiation requires.

Flat fees can be used for defined and predictable engagements, such as drafting a single contract, negotiating a specific deal, or in preparing a cease-and-desist letter. The advantage of a flat fee is budget certainty. The disadvantage is that it may not capture the full scope of attorney time if a transaction becomes more complex than anticipated. A well-drafted flat-fee engagement letter will define the scope with precision and specify what happens if that scope is exceeded.

Commission arrangements are less common for attorneys than for agents and managers, but they do exist, particularly in the context of attorneys who are actively involved in packaging projects or brokering transactions. The standard commission rate for an attorney acting in a transactional capacity is five percent of the deal, though some attorneys in this model charge as much as ten percent. Writers considering a commission arrangement with an attorney should understand clearly what they are getting for that commission and whether the attorney's involvement justifies it relative to an hourly or flat-fee alternative.

PRO TIP:

Many writers who are not yet represented by an agent use their entertainment attorney as their de facto dealmaker. The attorney reviews and negotiates every agreement, advises on which deals to accept and which to walk away from, and serves as the professional voice in the room when the writer cannot yet command one through agency representation.

Advantages: The attorney's ethical obligations are the strongest and most formally enforceable of any representative relationship. The attorney can be retained immediately, without threshold industry credentials, on a fee-for-service basis that does not require the attorney to believe in the writer's long-term commercial potential. The fee structure is transparent and negotiable. The attorney's interests, properly aligned through an appropriate engagement structure, are not complicated by commission incentives that favor deal closure over deal quality. And the attorney's review of every agreement is a protection that no other representative relationship provides as a primary function.

Disadvantages: The attorney does not, in most cases, provide the career development function of the manager or the market access function of the agent. Attorney fees, particularly on an hourly basis, can be substantial for writers who are in active transaction periods. And the attorney who is retained as a sole representative, without an agent or manager, leaves the writer without the submission access and relational infrastructure that the agent provides.

When Writers Turn to Attorneys

In the entertainment landscape, procuring legitimate agency representation can be difficult to obtain without a prior track record. The major agencies are not, as a practical matter, open to unsolicited submissions from unproduced writers. The mid-tier and boutique agencies are more accessible, but they too are selective. The result is a structural gap with a population of writers with completed, professional-quality material who cannot attract agency representation because they do not yet have the credits, the connections, or the professional visibility that agents require before taking on a new client. It's sort of like trying to get that first job out of college without any work experience.

In these instances, the entertainment attorney can serve a dual function. On the transactional side, the attorney can negotiate any agreement that comes to the writer. On the relational side, an experienced entertainment attorney who is connected in the independent film ecosystem can, without technically "procuring employment," facilitate introductions, identify opportunities, and create conditions that advance the writer's career.

The attorney who represents multiple production companies and independent financiers is not technically pitching the writer to those clients, but the attorney's awareness of both what the writer has and what the production company needs creates a context in which opportunities arise. Think of it as a matchmaker.

The writer who cannot yet attract an agent should be realistic about what the attorney can and cannot do. The attorney is not a substitute for agency representation in a guild context. The attorney cannot sign certain documents on the writer's behalf in the way an agent of record can. The attorney cannot pitch the writer's services to a major studio in a formal submission. What the attorney can do is protect the writer's interests in every transaction that does occur, ensure that no agreement is executed without proper review, and provide professional representation in negotiations that the writer would otherwise be conducting alone. Overall, the entertainment attorney adds professional legitimacy to the writer's team for optics and logistics.

How Representation Deals Work

The agreements that govern the relationships between writers and their representatives whether it is an agency agreement, a management agreement, or an attorney representation agreement, are themselves contracts that warrant the same careful attention the writer is encouraged to bring to every other agreement in their career. The instinct to sign whatever the representative provides out of gratitude or eagerness is a common mistake.

Each type of representative relationship is governed by a different form of agreement, subject to different regulatory constraints, and structured around different assumptions about term, commission, and termination. The following sections provide an analysis of how each works and what a writer should understand before executing any of them.

The Agency Agreement

In California, agency agreements are subject to the TAA and, for guild members, to the applicable guild franchise agreement. The WGA

Basic Agreement and the guild's Agency Regulations impose specific requirements on agency agreements. They must be in writing; they must specify the term and commission rate; and they must comply with guild provisions governing termination, exclusivity, and the agent's obligations to the talent. A WGA-franchised agency agreement that deviates from guild requirements is unenforceable to the extent of the deviation.

The standard WGA agency agreement is a relatively short document. The guild provides form agreements that franchised agencies are required to use for guild members. The key deal points are the term, the commission rate, the scope of representation (television, feature film, theatrical, or some combination), and the provisions governing termination and the post-termination tail.

Term and Termination—Agency agreements in the guild context typically run for one year, with mutual termination rights if the agency fails to procure employment within a specified period, historically ninety-one days, though this may vary by agreement and guild context. This "failure to procure" termination right is one of the most important protections in the standard guild agency agreement because it prevents a writer from being locked into an ineffective representation relationship indefinitely. Outside the guild context, agency agreement terms are negotiable, and the writer should resist long initial terms without meaningful termination rights.

Commission and the Tail—The commission for agents is typically ten percent of gross compensation on transactions procured by or as a result of the agent's efforts during the representation period. The *tail* provision, which is the period after termination during which the agent continues to receive commission on in-process transactions, is a meaningful point of negotiation. Tails of ninety days to one year are common. The writer should understand precisely what transactions are covered during the tail and whether the tail applies to renewals or extensions of deals that were in place at the time of termination.

The Management Agreement

Management agreements are private contracts, not subject to guild franchise requirements or TAA licensing in California. This gives both parties significant flexibility in structuring the relationship, which is both an opportunity and a risk. The flexibility means that management agreements can be tailored to the specific circumstances of the writer and the manager. It also means that a management agreement negotiated without attorney review may contain provisions that are highly disadvantageous to the writer and that have no regulatory check on their enforceability.

There are several historic cautionary tales in which managers have been accused of taking advantage of their clients, specifically in the case of Elvis Presley and his manager, Colonel Tom Parker, who reportedly took commissions as high as fifty percent. It was argued that their relationship was more collaborative than predatory, but the point remains that the manager-client relationship is virtually unregulated in the industry and thus the terms of the agreement should be carefully scrutinized.

> **PRO TIP:**
>
> Because there is no standard form management agreement in the way there is a standard form guild agency agreement, the agreement the manager sends you is the agreement the manager's attorney drafted to favor the manager. It should be reviewed by the writer's attorney before execution, and it should be negotiated.

Term and Termination—Management agreements commonly run for one to three years, with some managers seeking initial terms of up to five years for clients they are investing significant development time in. Unlike the guild agency agreement, there is typically no statutory or regulatory termination right for failure to procure employment. Termination rights in a management agreement are whatever the parties negotiate. The writer should insist on a termination right tied to meaningful performance benchmarks, or at minimum on a mutual termination right after a defined period with reasonable notice.

The post-termination tail in a management agreement can be significantly longer and broader than in an agency agreement. A manager who invested eighteen months developing a writer's project may argue for a commission on any transaction that results from that project, regardless of when it closes. This is a significant exposure, and the tail provision should be negotiated carefully: specify what transactions are covered, what the duration of the tail is, and whether the tail applies to sequel rights, remake rights, and other derivative transactions that may close years after termination.

The Producer Attachment Issue—Many managers, particularly those affiliated with production companies, will seek to attach themselves or their company as producers on any project they develop with the writer. A manager who adds genuine producing value may deserve a producer credit and the compensation that comes with it, but it creates a potential conflict of interest that the writer should understand before agreeing to it. The manager's interest as a producer may not always align perfectly with the writer's interest to retain creative control, protect separated rights, and maximize the writing fee. That tension is manageable, but it must be recognized and addressed in the management agreement.

Commission—The standard management commission of fifteen percent is calculated on gross compensation, typically including all writing fees, producing fees, and backend participation. Some management agreements include provisions for "gross deal" calculations that can expand the commission base beyond what the writer might expect. The commission base, the definition of gross compensation, and any carve-outs for transactions in which the manager was not involved should all be specified clearly in the agreement.

Attorney Representation

Attorney-client engagements are governed by state bar rules of professional conduct and, in California and in most states, by the State Bar Act and the Rules of Professional Conduct. These rules impose duties of loyalty, confidentiality, competence, and communication that provide the client with meaningful and enforceable protections that neither the agency nor the management relationship replicates. If an attorney breaches the duty of loyalty or acts against the client's interests, the client has recourse through the state bar disciplinary process, through legal malpractice litigation, or both.

The engagement is typically memorialized in an engagement letter or fee agreement, which specifies the scope of the representation, the fees, billing procedures, and the terms on which the engagement may be terminated by either party. California Rules of Professional Conduct Rule 1.5 requires that the basis or rate of the attorney's fee be communicated to the client in writing before or within a reasonable time after commencing the representation. A fee arrangement that is not in writing is not necessarily unenforceable, but it is a source of unnecessary risk for both parties.

Fee Structures—As previously mentioned, entertainment attorneys typically charge on an hourly, flat-fee, or commission basis, or some hybrid thereof. The engagement letter should specify which arrangement governs, what the rate or fee is, what is included in the scope of the representation, what is excluded, and how disputes about fees will be resolved. A true retainer is an advance payment against which hourly fees are billed and common for ongoing or open-ended representations. The retainer should be held in the attorney's client trust account, not commingled with the attorney's operating funds, a requirement imposed by professional responsibility rules.

For writers engaging an attorney on a transactional basis to review and negotiate a specific agreement a flat fee engagement is often the most budget-predictable structure. The writer knows in advance what the attorney's services will cost, can evaluate that cost against the value of the transaction, and can make an informed decision about whether to proceed.

The Attorney as Sole Representative

For writers who retain an attorney as their primary or sole professional representative the engagement letter should address the full scope of what the attorney will and will not do. The attorney can review every agreement, negotiate every deal, advise on rights strategy, and serve as the writer's representative in every transactional context. The attorney cannot, as a matter of California law, formally submit the writer for employment or hold themselves out as the writer's agent for procurement purposes without a TAA license.

That being said, the attorney who is well-connected in the independent film ecosystem can facilitate introductions without technically procuring employment. The attorney who represents multiple producers and financiers will naturally be aware of transactions in which the writer's services might be relevant. The attorney can advise on which opportunities to pursue and which to decline, negotiate the terms of any engagement that arises, and protect the writer's interests at every stage. What the attorney cannot do is replace the market access and submission authority that a licensed agent provides in the guild context.

The writer who understands the differences between the agent, manager, and attorney relationships clearly is positioned to assemble a professional team that serves their needs at their actual career stage. There is no universally correct combination. There is only the combination that is right for the specific writer, at the specific moment, in the specific market, with the right team players. That determination requires honest self-assessment, and it is worth making deliberately rather than by default.

ACT III

Getting the Project Off the Ground

Priya pitched her limited series concept to a production company after being introduced through a mutual contact. The company's head of development was enthusiastic and, in fact, he used the word "love" at least twice. At the end of the meeting, he had said that he wanted to "make something happen" and that he would "be in touch about next steps." Priya left the building convinced she was on the verge of her first real television deal.

What followed was six months of ambiguity that her attorney later described as a textbook case of informal attachment without documentation.

The development executive told colleagues about the project. He mentioned Priya's name in a meeting with a network executive. He had, by his own account, been "working on it." But there was no agreement, no terms discussed, and no shopping rights had been formally granted. After five months of unanswered emails, Priya submitted the same project through her newly signed manager to a different company, at which time the original production company sent a cease-and-desist letter asserting that she had granted them an exclusive right to develop the material.

She had not, but proving that by navigating the dispute, managing the professional fallout, and ultimately getting the project into the right hands took another eight months. It also cost her a directing attachment that had been contingent on a clean chain of title.

CHAPTER 7

PITCHING THE PROJECT

The previous chapter addressed the mechanics of professional representation and the distinctions between managers, agents, and attorneys; how commission structures work; and how to evaluate whether and when you need someone in your corner. This chapter addresses the pitch when your internal creative and business affairs become visible.

Pitching is the entertainment industry's primary mechanism for the exchange of creative ideas. Understanding what you are doing legally when you pitch, what you are sharing, what you are not protecting, and what you can and cannot do about it is imperative and it's the foundation on which your creative freedom is built.

What It Means to Pitch a Project

A pitch is an oral or visual presentation of a creative project, including the concept, characters, tone, and world, delivered to a buyer, financier, producer, studio, network, or streaming platform for the purpose of generating interest sufficient to justify a deal. The pitch is the conversation that precedes any of the agreements. When you execute a written agreement, you are operating inside a legal framework that governs the transfer of intellectual property rights. On the other hand, the pitch operates in a space that the law has deliberately left largely unregulated.

The practical reason is that creative industries depend on the free flow of ideas, and imposing legal formality on every preliminary creative conversation would bring development to a halt. The policy reason is that ideas alone are not protectable under copyright law. You cannot copyright an idea; you can only copyright the expression of an idea. You can copyright the specific characters, dialogue, plot structure, and creative choices that constitute a particular work fixed in a tangible medium. But the underlying concept belongs to no one. For example, you can't copyright a story about a woman who discovers her husband is living a double life, a workplace comedy set in a government agency, a prestige drama about the opioid crisis. Furthermore, the idea for your project when communicated orally in a pitch meeting is also not protectable intellectual property.

That reality has consequences that every writer should understand before she walks into a pitch meeting, posts a logline on a development forum, or describes her concept to a producer she met at a festival. It does not mean that the industry is a lawless environment where theft occurs with impunity. It means that the protections available to you are specific, limited, and largely dependent on the steps you take before the pitch.

The Fine Line Between Pitching and Submitting

Writers frequently use the words "pitch" and "submission" as though they were interchangeable, but they have different legal implications. A submission is the delivery of a written, fixed work, for example, a completed screenplay, a television pilot, a treatment, book proposal, or a series bible, to a prospective buyer or producer, typically in response to a solicitation or through the intermediary of representation. What you are submitting is a tangible, copyrightable expression whether it has been registered or not. When a company receives your submission, they are receiving your specific, protected expression of that concept. The laws governing that transaction, including an implied contract, the copyright protections attaching to your work, and the contractual terms of any release or submission agreement you may have signed, apply from the moment the document changes hands.

When you pitch, you are presenting ideas, concepts, story possibilities, and creative vision, sometimes supported by pitch materials. But for the most part, the pitch itself is an oral performance, and the ideas communicated in that performance are, by operation of law, unprotected as such. A submission can be tracked; a pitch often cannot. A submission generates a paper trail in the form of delivery confirmations, coverage notes, and pass letters that establishes when your material was received and by whom. A pitch frequently generates nothing but a zoom meeting or a networking event and, if you are fortunate, a follow-up email that may or may not accurately characterize what was said. A submission places the receiving party on formal notice of your authorship and the specific expression of your ideas. A pitch, unless accompanied by protective measures you have taken in advance, places them on notice of nothing beyond the general concept.

The implications for how you manage each type of encounter are, therefore, quite different. Material you submit should be registered with the U.S. Copyright Office before it goes out. Material you pitch should be accompanied by a written document that captures the core creative elements and establishes a contemporaneous record of your ownership.

What Materials Do You Submit

The materials you bring to a meeting, attach to an email, or upload to a portal are not interchangeable. Each one serves a different purpose, signals a different stage of development, and is appropriate for a different kind of project. Knowing which document to lead with, and which to hold in reserve, is part of presenting yourself as a professional rather than as someone learning the rules in real time. That being said, every producer works in their own way, and the rules are constantly changing. Zoom meetings are now the prevalent mode of first meetings. The materials below are the ones you are most likely to be asked for, in roughly the order they tend to be requested.

The Logline and One-Pager

The logline is a one- or two-sentence distillation of the project that captures the protagonist, the central conflict, and the stakes. The one-pager (sometimes called a one-sheet or leave-behind) expands that into a single page containing the title, genre, format, logline, a short synopsis, and a brief author bio. The one-pager is the document you send before anyone has agreed to read anything longer. It is also what an executive forwards others internally when they want to flag a project for a colleague.

The Treatment

A treatment is a prose summary of the story, written in present tense, that walks through the narrative from beginning to end. Treatments range from three to five pages on the short end to thirty or more pages on the long end. The treatment is most often used to test the story before a script is written, to communicate the shape of the project to a producer or financier early in development, or to support an option of an idea or concept that has not yet been written as a script. For original feature projects without an existing script, a treatment may be the lead document. For projects that already have a finished script, the treatment is rarely the lead.

The Pitch Deck

A pitch deck is a visual presentation, typically a PDF in landscape format built in Keynote, PowerPoint, or Canva, that combines images, mood references, character descriptions, tone, world-building, and a high-level synopsis into a single document designed to be read on a screen. Pitch decks have become standard for television projects, limited series, and high-concept features where tone, look, and world are central to the sell. The deck does not replace the script or the bible. It is the document that gets the meeting, supports the verbal pitch, and travels through an executive's inbox after the meeting ends.

The Series Bible

The bible is the foundational document for a television series. It typically includes the show's premise, tone, format, episode length, target platform, principal characters with full arcs, the world and its rules, the season-one-episode breakdowns, and a multi-season arc indicating where the series is headed. A bible is expected for any original television project being pitched seriously. For a limited series, the bible may also include a complete episode-by-episode beat-out for the full season. The bible is usually accompanied by a pilot script and a pitch deck.

The Pilot or Screenplay

The script is the fixed, copyrightable expression of the work and the document that ultimately determines whether the project gets made. For a feature, that means the screenplay. For a television series, it means the pilot. For a novel, that means the manuscript. The script is rarely the first document you send. It is the document a buyer asks for after the logline, one-pager, deck, or bible has generated enough interest to justify the read. When the script is requested, that is a meaningful signal of buyer interest.

Supporting Materials

Depending on the project, you may also be asked for or volunteer additional materials such as character breakdowns, look books, sizzle reels or proof-of-concept shorts, comparable-title analysis, budget ranges, or attachments confirming director, producer, or talent interest. These are meant to supplement the core materials, not replace them.

Which Materials You Lead With

The right lead document depends on the type of project and where it is in development. For an original feature with a completed script, the typical sequence is logline, one-pager, then script on request. A pitch deck is optional and most useful for high-concept, visually distinctive material. However, given the ease of design platforms now available, it is advisable to create a pitch deck for any project. This is a visual industry with visual creatives and executives making the decisions.

For an original feature without a completed script, you are pitching an idea rather than a finished work. The lead documents are typically a treatment and a pitch deck, sometimes accompanied by a short writing sample that demonstrates voice. You should be candid that the script is not yet written; representing otherwise creates problems later.

For an original television series, the standard package is a pitch deck, a series bible, and a pilot script. The deck and a brief verbal pitch are what get the meeting. The bible and pilot are what the buyer reads after the meeting if they are interested.

For a limited series, the package is similar to a series bible package, with the bible expanded to include episode-by-episode beats for the full season, since a limited series is sold as a single complete story rather than an open-ended franchise.

For an adaptation, whether of a book, article, podcast, or other underlying work, the lead document is typically a pitch deck or treatment that articulates your specific take, paired with evidence that you control or can control the underlying rights. Without that evidence, no buyer will engage seriously, regardless of how strong the creative materials are.

For an unscripted or reality format, the lead document is a format bible or format deck that describes the show's premise, structure, episode template, and distinctive elements, often supported by a sizzle reel demonstrating tone and casting.

The practical rule across all of these is to lead with the shortest document that conveys what is distinctive about the project, and to send longer materials only when they are requested. A buyer who wants more will ask. A buyer who is sent a 110-page screenplay before they have decided whether they are interested in the premise will not read it. Whatever materials you send out, register them with the U.S. Copyright Office before they leave your hands. Pitch decks, treatments, series bibles, and pilot scripts are each independently copyrightable as literary or visual works, and the modest filing fee buys you a dated, government-issued record of authorship that becomes invaluable if a question of who created the materials arises later.

Contests and Film Festivals

The past decade has seen a significant increase in pitch competitions at film festival panels, television market pitch sessions, and industry showcase events at which writers are invited to present their projects to panels of judges who may include producers, executives, and financiers. The appeal of the pitch panel is access to industry professionals.

An emerging writer who has not yet secured representation can stand in front of a Sundance development executive, a Tribeca producer, or a CAA represented manager and pitch her project directly, often in a format specifically designed to encourage that kind of early-stage creative exposure. Festival pitch events, such as the Sundance Institute labs, Austin Film Festival's pitch sessions, the Cannes Marché du Film, and the Series Mania Forum, have generated genuine career-launching deals. However, they present a specific set of risks that are worth discussing.

First, before you participate in any formal pitch program, you should read the submission and participation agreement with care. Some of these agreements include provisions that are broadly worded releases of claims arising from the use of submitted or pitched material, grants of rights to use pitch materials for promotional or educational purposes, and waivers of certain legal claims that might otherwise be available if your concept were subsequently developed without your involvement. None of these provisions are necessarily disqualifying, but they should be reviewed before you automatically agree. At the least, have clear expectations as to the exchange involved.

Second, the panel format creates a specific problem. When you pitch to a room full of industry professionals, you are presenting your concept simultaneously to multiple parties, many of whom you do not know, none of whom have signed any agreement with you specifically. Not to mention the audience members in attendance. You are pitching your idea in a public or semi-public setting, and the law will not extend protection to that idea merely because the context was a competitive event.

Third, festival and competition pitch formats are frequently too brief to allow you to establish the specificity and creative particularity that might otherwise distinguish your protectable expression from the general concept. A three-minute pitch, or a ten-minute panel presentation, often succeeds by communicating the most compelling and universal elements of a project. The aspects of your work that are most protectable such as your specific characters, your particular plotting choices, your distinctive narrative voice, are often the aspects that cannot be communicated effectively in the time available, nor may you want to disclose them in a public forum.

None of this should discourage you from pitching at festivals and competitions. These events remain among the most valuable opportunities available to unrepresented writers for the reasons noted above. The point is simply that you should enter them with clear eyes about what the experience does and does not protect, and with the following minimum precautions in place: *your underlying written material should be registered with the U.S. Copyright Office before the event*. You should have a brief written document even if only a one-page that accompanies or follows up on your pitch and establishes a contemporaneous paper trail.

PRO TIP:

Before publicly releasing your project whether online or in a public forum such as a pitch festival or contest, register your work with the U.S. Copyright Office, including your pitch deck, treatment, and script, at whatever stage it's currently in of development.

How to Protect Yourself When Pitching

The most reliable way to ensure that your creative expression is protected at the time of a pitch is to have already fixed it in a tangible medium, registered that fixed expression, and positioned yourself to demonstrate, if necessary, that your specific creative choices predate any subsequent development by the party to whom you pitched.
In practice, this means the following.

- **Register your underlying material before it leaves your hands.** If you have a completed screenplay, register it with the U.S. Copyright Office and log it with the WGA. If you have a treatment, a series bible, a detailed outline, a collection of scene breakdowns, then register those too. Copyright registration provides you with a date-stamped public record of the existence and content of your specific expression at a specific moment in time. It is cheap, fast, and it is the most fundamental protective act available to you. There is no legitimate reason not to do it before any material goes out.
- **Prepare a brief written document to accompany or follow up on your pitch.** A one-page, a short treatment, or a pitch

deck serves multiple purposes simultaneously. It functions as a marketing tool, reinforcing the creative impression you made in the room. It functions as a communication device, ensuring that the party you pitched understands your concept accurately. And it functions as a legal record, establishing in writing what you presented and when. A follow-up email that summarizes the key elements of your pitch and thanks the recipient for their time.

- **Understand submission releases before you sign them.** Many production companies and studios will not accept unsolicited submissions without a signed release agreement. This document typically limits your legal remedies if the company subsequently develops a project that resembles your submission. These releases are common, they are generally enforceable, and they are not per se unreasonable. Companies receive enormous volumes of submissions and must protect themselves against frivolous claims from writers who mistake coincidence for theft. Believe it or not, as much as you might be worried about someone stealing your idea, companies are equally worried about being accused of stealing your work. For these reasons, production companies often require a representative, such as an agent or entertainment attorney, to make the submission on your behalf. If you are asked to sign a submission release, read it carefully before you do. If you do not understand it, ask an attorney to review it. And note carefully whether the release applies to the general concept you are pitching or only to the specific material you are submitting.
- **Maintain your own records.** Keep a log of every pitch you make. Include the date, the venue, the participants, the project presented, and the substance of what was discussed. Keep copies of all written materials you leave behind. Retain all correspondence, emails, messages, and follow-ups that relate to the pitch. These records will give you an evidentiary foundation

from which to pursue any claim that could arise, and they will establish your credibility and seriousness if a dispute were to arise, not to mention a good system for your own submission records.

The Myth of the Stolen Idea

There is a belief that pervades writers' rooms, festival lounges, and online screenwriting communities that idea theft is rampant in Hollywood, that executives routinely steal concepts from writers they meet in pitch meetings, and that the pitch is a fundamentally dangerous transaction in which the writer is the inevitable victim.

The reality is that the phenomenon by which two or more creators develop similar ideas simultaneously and without knowledge of each other is not only possible but statistically inevitable. The entertainment industry operates within a cultural moment. Projects get greenlit in clusters because they respond to the same cultural anxieties, the same demographic trends, the same news cycles. When a story about artificial intelligence appears on one streaming platform six months after a writer pitched a story about artificial intelligence to that same platform, the best explanation is not theft. It's that multiple people, responding to the same cultural stimulus, arrived at similar creative conclusions at roughly the same time. This happens constantly, and it is why Hollywood periodically releases three volcano movies in the same calendar year.

The legal doctrines governing idea theft claims reflect this reality. To prevail on an implied contract theory, a plaintiff must establish not only that her idea was disclosed and used, but that there was an implied promise to pay if the idea was used and that the idea was novel and concrete enough to support such a claim. This was the standard set forth following the California Supreme Court's decision in *Desny v. Wilder*, 46 Cal. 2d 715 (1956) and prevails today. Courts have consistently held that general concepts, premises, and themes do not meet it. The more general your pitch, the more difficult it becomes to establish that the subsequent development you are challenging actually used your specific creative contribution rather than an idea that was independently generated or already in common circulation.

None of this means that idea theft never occurs. There are documented cases, some of which have resulted in substantial judgments against studios and production companies. But those cases share a common characteristic wherein the plaintiff could point to specific, protectable creative elements, detailed characters, particular plot structures, distinctive narrative devices that appeared in the allegedly infringing work and could be traced to materials she had created and shared. In other words, the plaintiff was able to prove copyright infringement based on previously created copyrighted materials.

The practical implication is that paranoia about idea theft is not a substitute for proper documentation. The writer who is too afraid to pitch will never gain traction on their project, short of being their own producer and making it themselves.

The Benefits of Having Representation

Consider the practical differences between pitching with representation and pitching without it. When you pitch without representation, you are typically doing so through whatever informal access you have been able to create for yourself, perhaps a connection made at a festival, a mutual contact, a cold query that happened to land in a sympathetic inbox. You do not know the standard terms of a pitch deal at that company. You do not know whether the executive with whom you are meeting has the authority to green light a project, the interest to follow up on one, or the track record to be trusted with your material. You are pitching into an informational vacuum, relying on your instincts about people and situations you have no independent means of evaluating.

When you pitch with representation, the landscape is fundamentally different. Your representative has a pre-existing relationship with the company you are pitching. She knows the executive's taste, the company's development slate, their current acquisitions priorities, and the terms they typically offer on option agreements. She knows whether the company has a reputation for honorable dealing or for tying up material and sitting on it. She will, in many cases, have negotiated deals with this company before and will know where there is flexibility and where there is not. Before you walk into the room, she has done reconnaissance that would take you years to replicate independently.

Representation also solves, or substantially mitigates, the submission release problem. A company that will not accept unsolicited submissions from an unrepresented writer will typically accept submissions from a known, established agent or manager without requiring a broad release agreement. The submission arrives pre-vetted, pre-credentialed, and within a relationship that imposes its own informal norms of professional conduct. The formal legal protections that a submission release is designed to provide are partly supplanted by the reputational and relational dynamics of the industry's network of ongoing professional relationships.

And if something does go wrong, say you pitch your project and six months later a similar project appears in development, your representative is in a far better position than you are to make a discreet inquiry to assess what actually happened and advise you on whether the situation warrants any response. She has experience to distinguish between independent development and actual misappropriation that may not otherwise be objectively obvious.

This is not an argument that unrepresented writers should not pitch. They should, and they will, and some of them will close deals. The protections available to a writer in the pitch context are not solely legal in nature, they are relational and representation is the mechanism by which those protections are accessed. In turn, the writer is better positioned to pitch with confidence, to negotiate with clarity, and to build the kind of long-term professional relationships that constitute a sustainable career in this industry. In the best cases, the pitch phase is the beginning of a professional collaboration that will outlast any single project. Approaching it with the sophistication it demands from the beginning is the foundation on which that magic is built.

CHAPTER 8

PRODUCER ATTACHMENTS

The producer attachment is one of the most misunderstood transactions in the entertainment industry. Writers encounter producers at festivals, through mutual contacts, through query letters and cold outreach, and through the referral networks that develop around any active professional community. Many of those producers are talented, well-intentioned, and genuinely positioned to advance a project. Some are not. And others are enthusiastic, connected, but have not yet demonstrated whether their enthusiasm and connections are sufficient to get a project made.

This chapter addresses what producers actually do as opposed to the industry's frequently mythologized account of the producer's role. It addresses the critical distinction between shopping a project and producing it, and why that distinction carries significant legal consequences for the writer.

> **PRO TIP:**
>
> Research a producer's IMDb profile to see past, current, and future projects to get an accurate track record.

What Producers Actually Do

The title "producer" is among the most arbitrary roles in the entertainment industry. It is a title that anyone can claim and whose actual contributions vastly range from creative and logistical leadership to the procurement of casting talent. The WGA, the DGA, the Producers Guild, and the major studios have all, at various points and with varying degrees of success, attempted to impose some definitional discipline on the producer credit.

For purposes of agreements you may encounter and be asked to sign, it is useful to distinguish among three functional categories of producer, understanding that the same individual may move among them depending on the project and the stage of development.

> **The producing producer** is the person who actually makes the film or television project by assembling the financing, hiring the director and key crew, overseeing physical production, managing the budget, solving the problems that arise between a script and a finished project, and delivering the completed work to a distributor. This is the producer whose attachment to a project meaningfully increases its likelihood of getting made. She has infrastructure, including a production company with overhead, relationships with financiers, a track record of completed projects, and the operational capacity to move a script through development, financing, and production. This attachment is valuable and also relatively rare at the stage when most writers are first approached by a producer.

> **The development producer** is the person who works with writers and material in the earlier, pre-financing phase of a project to help identify scripts, develop relationships with talent, shape a project creatively, and position it for the conversations that may eventually lead to financing

and production. A development producer with strong relationships at studios, networks, or streaming platforms, a reputation for identifying strong material early, and the ability to package a project compellingly is a real asset to a writer who does not yet have access to those relationships independently. The question to ask about a development producer is not whether she is talented but whether her specific relationships and track record are likely to translate into actual production and on what timeline.

The shopping producer is the person whose primary contribution is taking your material out by making calls, setting meetings, and attempting to interest buyers in a project that she does not have the independent capacity to finance or produce herself. She is operating as an introducer, a connector, a door-opener. It's important to know that a shopping producer is not a producing producer, and the attachment agreement she is offering you is not an option, a purchase agreement, or a development deal. It is an agreement granting her the right to use your material as an introduction.

None of these categories is inherently better or worse than the others. What matters is that you understand which category a prospective producer occupies before you attach her to your project, and that the terms of any attachment agreement you sign accurately reflect the scope and limitations of what she is going to do. A shopping agreement with a well-connected shopping producer, on fair terms, with appropriate protections, is a legitimate transaction. The same agreement misrepresented as something more substantive is a trap.

Before signing any producer attachment agreement, you should therefore be able to answer the following questions. What has this producer produced, and what was the outcome of those projects?

What specific relationships does she have at the buyers most relevant to your material, and how current and active are those relationships? What is her plan for this specific project, and what concrete steps does she propose to take, on what timeline? Does she have the resources and infrastructure to develop the project, or is she dependent on selling it in order to generate the resources to develop it? And perhaps most importantly what happens to your project if she is unable to set it up within the term of the agreement?

Shopping or Producing a Script?

The distinction between shopping a script and producing it is the distinction between two fundamentally different legal and commercial transactions, each with different implications for your rights, your timeline, and your ability to do anything else with your material while the agreement is in effect.

When a producer shops a script, she is presenting your material to third-party buyers, i.e. studios, networks, streamers, financiers, in an attempt to generate an offer that will enable her to attach herself to the project as a producer and move it toward production. She does not, at this stage, own any rights in your script. She has been granted, by the terms of the shopping agreement, a limited and typically exclusive right to use your material for this purpose during a defined period. If she succeeds in attracting a buyer, the buyer's acquisition of the underlying rights and the terms on which your script is purchased or optioned will be governed by a separate agreement negotiated at that time. The shopping agreement itself does not transfer your rights; it governs the producer's authority to seek a buyer.

When a producer produces a project, the legal structure is different in kind. Production requires that the producer (or the entity financing the project) control the rights necessary to make the film or television program. That control is typically established through an option-purchase agreement, a literary purchase agreement, or a work-for-hire arrangement, depending on the nature of the underlying material and the writer's role going forward. These agreements, which will be discussed in more detail later, transfer rights, impose obligations, and create the legal foundation on which a production can be financed and insured.

The practical problem arises in the space between these two transactions after the shopping agreement has been signed but before any buyer has made a formal offer, during which the producer is actively presenting your material and you are, by the terms of the agreement, unable to present it to anyone else. This is what's meant by *exclusivity*. This period can last months, if not years, depending on the terms of the agreement. The legal and commercial consequences for the writer are significant in ways that are not always apparent from the face of the agreement.

Consider what exclusivity means in this context. A shopping agreement that grants the producer an exclusive right to shop your script during its term prevents you from taking your material to any buyer she has not already approached, from responding to inbound interest from buyers who contact you independently, and from negotiating with the producer with different terms once you have learned more about the market's interest in your project. If a competing producer with stronger relationships, a better track record, or an active financing relationship expresses interest in your material during the exclusive shopping period, you cannot engage with her. The exclusivity provision has removed your ability to capitalize on that interest, regardless of how attractive it may be. Or if the agreement allows you to simultaneously shop the project, the original producer will still likely remain attached to the project even if in the form of a credit.

This is why the term of the shopping agreement is one of the most important provisions you will negotiate. An exclusive shopping right of six months, with one optional extension of three months exercisable only upon payment of additional consideration, is a very different transaction from an exclusive shopping right of eighteen months with automatic renewal provisions that can extend the exclusivity period indefinitely. The former gives the producer a reasonable but finite window to demonstrate what she can do with your material. The latter can tie up your project for years without any meaningful obligation on the producer's part to actually produce anything.

Several additional protections deserve attention in any shopping agreement negotiation. First, the agreement should specify the buyers to whom the producer is authorized to submit the material or, at minimum, impose a notification obligation requiring her to inform you of each submission. This is not only a transparency measure, but it protects you from the scenario in which a producer submits your material to every significant buyer in the market, generates a series of passes, and effectively exhausts the project's commercial prospects during the shopping period. A script that has been submitted to every major studio and streamer and passed on by each of them is materially harder to set up than a script that has not yet been widely circulated. You should know, in real time, where your material is going.

Second, the agreement should address what happens to any offer that the producer generates during the shopping period. The producer's authority under a shopping agreement is typically limited to soliciting interest and presenting offers. She does not have the authority to accept an offer on your behalf, commit you to any terms, or transfer any rights without your approval. This limitation should be explicit in the agreement, not implied. The producer is your representative in a limited sense and for a limited purpose; she is not your agent, she does not have authority to bind you to any transaction, and any offer she receives should be transmitted to you promptly and in full.

Third, the agreement should specify what happens to the producer's attachment if a deal is not closed during the shopping period. Does the producer's right to a producer credit on any subsequent production survive the expiration of the shopping agreement? Does she retain any right to compensation if you later sell the project to a buyer she introduced you to during the shopping period? These provisions vary, and their implications are significant. A producer who retains a credit or compensation right beyond the expiration of her shopping agreement has, in effect, created a long-term financial obligation that attaches to your project regardless of whether she does any further work on it. This can create a dead weight effect particularly for the future producer. It's wise to always know who you're getting in business with because after the divorce, so to speak, you may still have to raise the children together.

When Producers Ask for Rights Too Early

The most likely next step that you will encounter is to formalize your relationship with a producer in the form of a shopping agreement or option purchase agreement, the terms of which the chapters that follow will address in detail. A producer who asks instead for something that functions like a rights transfer with broad exclusivity, the authority to attach herself as a producer, the right to negotiate with buyers on your behalf, or the right to bind you to terms should be a red flag. This type of request could come in many forms, such as an informal attachment letter, a "memorandum of understanding," a "letter of intent," or simply as "something for my files." The document may be short and may be written in language that sounds more conversational than contractual. It should not be evaluated by its length or its tone but by its operative provisions.

Another arrangement that warrants a red flag is any producer who conditions their attachment on an upfront fee for services. As a general matter, producers in the entertainment industry are compensated on the back end through a producing fee paid at commencement of principal photography, through profit participation, or through some combination of the two.

A producer who asks to be paid before the project has been sold, greenlit, or financed is, in effect, asking you to bear all the financial risk regardless of their continued involvement. It's a pay to play arrangement, which such a producer may provide a compelling argument that this is the only way to get your project made. However, this is not how legitimate producing relationships are structured, and it is a pattern that should prompt serious inquiry before any agreement is signed. I've seen more than one client (who comes to me for representation after the fact) enter into such an arrangement to only be disappointed by the results. The bottom line is you want to partner with someone who believes in the project, not who is looking to get paid on the front end and then bail. It's easy to confuse the enthusiasm they exude for your project when it's really for the payment they will be receiving.

The narrow exception to this principle is where the producer is being engaged to deliver a specific, tangible work product as part of the development process, such as a professionally produced pitch deck, a sizzle reel, a lookbook, a budget breakdown, or similar materials that require out-of-pocket expenditure or specialized expertise. In those circumstances, a fee tied to actual deliverable materials is defensible, provided the scope of work is clearly defined, the fee is proportionate to the deliverable, and the agreement specifies what rights you retain in those materials if the relationship does not proceed. Even then, review the arrangement carefully. A fee structured around deliverables can still be used as a vehicle for extracting payment without meaningful reciprocal obligation, particularly if the deliverables are defined vaguely, valued arbitrarily, or conditioned on your continued engagement with that producer. The deliverable should justify the fee, not the other way around.

PRO TIP:

If you are paying for deliverables, then it should be done under a work for hire arrangement in which you will own the materials.

The critical questions to ask of any producer attachment document, regardless of what it is called, are the following: Does it grant any form of exclusivity, and if so, for how long and over what scope of transactions? Does it convey any rights in your material, or does it merely authorize the producer to present it? Does it create any obligations that survive the expiration of the document? Does it contain any provision that would automatically extend its term, whether through a renewal option, a "negotiation period," a right of first refusal on any subsequent deal, or even an overly broad force majeure provision?

Each of these provisions, if present, represents a meaningful encumbrance on your rights that should be negotiated with full awareness of its implications rather than accepted because the document appeared harmless on first reading. As already discussed, the rights in a project are the fundamental currency of every transaction. Every agreement you sign that involves your creative material is, at its core, an agreement about who controls what rights, for how long, and under what conditions. The producer who asks you to sign an attachment agreement before she has demonstrated the capability, the relationships, and the commitment that would justify a rights transfer is asking you to spend that currency before you have received any consideration in return.

Simply put, before you sign any producer attachment document, however informal it appears (especially, if it appears informal), have it reviewed by an entertainment attorney who reads these documents regularly, understands the industry norms against which their terms should be evaluated, and can tell you with specificity what you are agreeing to and what you are giving up.

Producers are among the most important creative and professional collaborators a writer can have, and the relationship between a writer and a producer who are genuinely aligned on a project is one of the most generative in the industry. The point of this chapter is not to make you suspicious of every producer who expresses interest in your work but to ensure that when you formalize that relationship you do so from a position of informed understanding rather than grateful deference. The producers who are worth attaching to your project will respect that position and the ones who do not are telling you something important about the deal you are actually being offered.

ACT IV

The Agreements That Drive the Industry

Terrence wrote a feature script that had generated genuine interest. Two production companies wanted it, and one of them moved quickly. The producer was experienced, well-regarded, and spoke highly of the script. The agreement he sent was ten pages. It had defined terms and proper recitals and looked, to Terrence's untrained eye, like a serious legal document negotiated in good faith. His manager glanced at it and said it looked "pretty standard."

It was standard, and that was the problem.

Standard shopping agreements are drafted to protect the producer. The shopping period was twelve months with a twelve-month renewal at the producer's sole election. The definition of "Project" included not just the screenplay but all prior drafts, the treatment, any pitch materials, and the underlying concept. The scope was broad enough to effectively tie up any version of the story Terrence might want to tell. There was no reversion mechanism tied to the producer's activity level. There was no requirement that the producer make any minimum efforts.

Two years later, the project had not been set up anywhere, the producer had stopped returning calls, and Terrence had no contractual basis to demand the rights back. The agreement had not expired. It had not been breached in any way he could point to. It had given the producer every option and left Terrence with the downside.

CHAPTER 9

DEVELOPMENT AGREEMENTS

Before examining each type of agreement individually, it's worth understanding how they relate to one another on a continuum of commitment. At one end is the shopping agreement, which conveys the least and obligates the least. At the other end is the option–purchase agreement, which conveys the rights necessary to produce the underlying work upon payment of a pre-determined purchase price. The stand-alone option agreement sits somewhere in between the two. Understanding where on that continuum any given offer falls is the first consideration.

The second thing to understand is that the name a producer gives an agreement is not controlling. Producers (and occasionally their attorneys) often use these terms imprecisely, calling something an "option" when it's actually a shopping agreement, or describing a purchase agreement as an "option" because the word sounds less final. Never judge an agreement by its title. Instead, read the operative provisions and identify what rights the agreement conveys, for how long, at what cost to the producer, and at what risk to you.

The Shopping Agreement

A shopping agreement (sometimes called a submission release, a shopping release, or simply an "agreement") is basically a permission from the writer to the producer or interested buyer. The writer grants the producer the right to present the material to third parties, typically studios, networks, streaming platforms, or financiers, for a defined period of time, for the purpose of soliciting interest in developing, producing, or financing the project. It does not convey a purchase right, nor obligate the producer to pay the writer anything, either now or upon exercise. Except for possibly creating pitch materials, it does not give the producer the right to develop, alter, or produce the work. It is, in essence, a limited authorization to shop the project on the writer's behalf.

The consideration for a shopping agreement is typically the producer's promise to use commercially reasonable efforts to exploit the material in exchange for the producer's future attachment to the project. In practice, this means the agreement may be entered into without any upfront payment from the producer (or to the producer). Any reference to money for either writer or producer is contemplated and negotiated in a future agreement with the third party that the producer has brought into the fold. The writer provides the material (ideally, copyrighted material); the producer provides the promise of efforts. Whether those efforts materialize is essentially a gamble of time for both parties.

When a Writer Encounters It

Shopping agreements are most common at the earliest stages of a project's commercial life before the material has attracted any significant institutional attention and before the producer has the resources or inclination to pay for a formal option. The shopping agreement is the most common choice for independent producers without development funds, producers who are themselves emerging and testing the market for a project, and producers who are not yet certain they believe in the material enough to pay for it. A writer approached by a producer with a shopping agreement is, for all practical purposes, being approached by a producer who is not yet willing to commit capital to the project.

That observation is not necessarily a reason to decline. Some of the most significant productions in film and television began their commercial life under a shopping arrangement. The relevant question is not whether the producer is willing to pay, but whether the producer has genuine access to the buyers and decision-makers who can move the project forward, and whether the terms of the shopping agreement adequately protect the writer during the period in which that access is being exercised.

The Writer's Risk

The primary risk a shopping agreement poses to the writer is the loss of time. Because the producer pays nothing upfront, there is no sunk cost motivating the producer to work expeditiously. A shopping agreement that runs twelve months, with an option to extend, can tie up a project for a year or more while the producer makes only casual efforts. In the meantime, the writer cannot take the project elsewhere. At the end of the shopping period, if no deal has materialized, the writer receives the project back exactly as she gave it: unsold, with a development history that may or may not be helpful depending on which doors the producer opened and which doors he closed.

The other risk worth noting is reputational. A producer who presents material poorly to the wrong buyers, framed incorrectly, without the relationships to get it read seriously can damage the project's market position in ways that a subsequent producer will have to overcome. The project that has already been submitted to every major studio and rejected without a serious conversation is a harder project to revive than one that has been strategically withheld.

The Option Agreement

An option agreement is fundamentally different from a shopping agreement, even though the two are sometimes confused in casual usage. Where a shopping agreement grants only a permission to present the project, an option agreement grants something of considerably greater legal significance: the exclusive right to purchase the underlying work within a defined time period and at a price to be determined. The producer does not acquire the work at the moment the option is signed. Instead, she has the right to acquire it on future terms to be agreed upon.

The option payment is the price the producer pays to hold the right of first refusal on the project for the duration of the option period. That payment may be nominal or substantial, ranging from one dollar to thousands of dollars and it may be applicable against the purchase price, or it may not. But the existence of an option payment, even a small one, is one of the features that distinguishes a true option agreement from a shopping arrangement dressed up in option language. A producer who pays for an option has made a financial commitment, however modest, to the project.

The Mechanics of Exercise

During the option period, the producer typically has the right to develop the project by attaching elements, seeking financing, pitching buyers, and generally advancing the project toward production, subject to whatever limitations the option agreement imposes on modifications to the underlying work. If, before the option period expires, the producer decides to move forward, she "exercises" the option. Exercise converts the producer's contractual right into an executed transfer of rights. The terms of that transfer include the purchase price, the rights conveyed, the credits, and the backend participation that may have been negotiated within the option agreement itself.

If the option period expires without exercise, the rights revert to the writer and the producer retains nothing. If properly negotiated, the producer does not retain the development work product, nor any attachment to the project. The option payment is typically non-refundable, and the writer keeps the money. In summary, the producer pays for the right to hold the project for a defined time and if the option isn't exercised, then the payment is forfeited and the rights revert back to the rightsholder. As such, the writer is compensated for the time the project is off the market.

When a Writer Encounters It

Option agreements arise when a producer has a genuine and financially substantiated interest in the material but is not yet in a position to commit to an outright purchase. If the work is in a leveraged position, then the producer may need to use an option agreement rather than a shopping agreement to lure the writer with compensation. And yet, projects take a team of people to develop which takes time. The option buys that time and it also makes it a lucrative proposition for the writer or rightsholder. Thus, the option is a common agreement used for projects that have attracted meaningful producer attention but have not yet been set up at a studio or financed for production. Independent films, prestige television projects, and adaptations of non-bestselling source material are frequently optioned rather than purchased outright, because the producer needs time to attach a director, find a co-producer with studio access, or secure development financing before committing to a full acquisition price.

A writer receiving a stand-alone option agreement without the purchase terms, should treat that as an incomplete document. The option payment and the option period are only two of the relevant deal points. If the purchase terms are not fixed at the time the option is signed, the writer has agreed to let the producer hold the project for a defined period without knowing what she will be paid if the producer ultimately exercises. That is a significant concession, and it is one that writers frequently make without realizing they have done so. That being said, once there are third party attachments, then the purchase price may justify a higher price than when the option was entered. Alternatively, the opposite could happen.

Let's say a writer signs a stand-alone option agreement at a time when the producer is interested, but no studio has committed, no director is attached, and the project's commercial prospects are unproven. The option runs eighteen months. Toward the end of that period, the producer has attached a major director, a studio has expressed acquisition interest, and the project is suddenly a commercial proposition worth many times its original value. The producer now wants to exercise. But the purchase terms were never agreed upon. Who has the most leverage now? The producer's leverage is now arguably greater than it was at the time of the original option because of how well he has positioned the project. As a result, the writer negotiates the purchase terms from a position of surprise, urgency, and imbalance. Of course, now an argument can be made that the writer has more leverage because the value of the project is more transparent than before. If the writer is represented, this is certainly the best position to take in negotiating the purchase price.

An option purchase agreement eliminates that dynamic entirely. The purchase terms are fixed at the moment of maximum ambiguity, which is also, not coincidentally, the moment at which the writer's leverage is at its most equal. Once the deal is set, it does not matter whether the project subsequently becomes worth more or less than its agreed purchase price. Both parties are bound to the terms they negotiated. That is the fundamental value of the option purchase and why it is advisable over the stand-alone option.

The Option Purchase Agreement

The option purchase agreement is the most complete of the three instruments. It combines the option mechanism with a fully negotiated and binding purchase agreement that will automatically govern the acquisition of rights if and when the option is exercised. It is, in essence, two agreements in one document: (1) a present agreement to hold the project under option, and (2) a future agreement to purchase it that becomes operative upon exercise. The purchase terms, along with the rights conveyed, the credits, the reversion rights, and the backend structure, are negotiated and memorialized now, not deferred to a future negotiation that may never occur or that may occur under conditions less favorable to the writer.

Option purchase agreements are the standard contract used by studios, production companies with active development slates, and any producer sophisticated enough to know what they are doing. It is more work to negotiate on the front end and therefore more costly in terms of legal fees. It requires both parties to reach agreement on the purchase terms before anyone knows whether the option will ever be exercised. But that front-end work is precisely what makes the instrument fair and functional. It ensures that both parties know, at the moment of signing, what they have agreed to. The writer knows what she will receive if the producer exercises and the producer knows what it will cost to acquire the project. If a producer presents you with an option without the purchase terms, or it defers the purchase negotiation to a future date, then it is entirely appropriate for you or your attorney to request that the purchase terms be incorporated into the current agreement.

The following summary is intended for reference only. The specific terms of any given agreement will govern, and no generalization should substitute for a careful review of the actual instrument.

Feature	**Shopping Agreement**	**Option Agreement**	**Option–Purchase Agreement**
Upfront Payment	Rarely; if ever	Yes, option fee paid	Yes, option fee paid
Purchase Terms Fixed?	No	Deferred	Yes, at signing

Feature	Shopping Agreement	Option Agreement	Option–Purchase Agreement
Rights Conveyed Now	Permission to shop only	Right to exercise the option	Right to exercise + fixed purchase terms
Development Rights?	Depends	Usually yes, within limits	Yes, within agreed limits
Writer Risk	Time off market; no payment	Time off market; purchase terms TBD	Time off market; terms known upfront
Producer Commitment	Minimal; effort-based only	Financial (option fee)	Financial + contractually bound purchase
Typical Context	Early stage; emerging producers	Mid-development; serious interest	Established producers; studio-level deals

Knowing What Is Actually Being Offered

Whenever a producer approaches you with a development agreement, the first question is to identify which of these three agreements you are actually being offered, not what the producer calls it, what the cover email says, or even what the title of the agreement says.

Is there an upfront payment? If not, why not, and what is the producer committing to in exchange for your granting them exclusivity? Are the purchase terms fixed? If not, when will they be negotiated, under what process, and what happens if the parties cannot agree? How long does the agreement run, and on what terms can it be extended? What rights does the producer have during the option period to develop or modify the material? What happens to the development work product if the option expires unexercised?

These questions will be examined in detail in the chapters that follow. The major deal points, including the option price, the purchase price, the term, the reversion triggers, the credit provisions, the backend structure, are each subject of their own analysis. But none of that analysis is useful if you do not first know what kind of agreement you are being asked to sign.

The entertainment industry moves quickly, and producers often present agreements with a sense of urgency that, whether intentional or not, pressures a writer's deliberation time. However, resist the urgency. A producer who is genuinely committed to the project will not walk away because you took a week to review the agreement with counsel. And if they do, then you have your answer to also walk away.

CHAPTER 10

RIGHTS TRANSFER AGREEMENTS

What happens once the option has been exercised? Or perhaps the studio has made a direct offer on your script, or a streaming platform wants to acquire the underlying rights to your novel outright, without an option at all. What differs now from the scenarios in the previous chapter is that now a party with resources wants to permanently acquire the rights. In this case, a literary purchase agreement, a license (which also includes a book publishing agreement), or an assignment is the most consequential document you will sign in the life cycle of any given project. It is the document that determines not only what you will be paid, but what you will retain, what you will lose, and what leverage, if any, you will have over the work for the rest of its commercial life.

The terminology matters here in ways it does not always matter elsewhere. A license and an assignment are not interchangeable. A literary purchase agreement is not simply a longer option. Understanding the legal distinction between these contracts and what each one does is the foundation for this chapter and those that follow.

Rights Transfer and the Copyright Bundle

Before examining each agreement individually, it's important to note that all three of these documents are, at their core, mechanisms for moving some or all the pieces of the copyright bundle from the writer (or current rightsholder) to another party. Chapter One of this book introduced the concept of copyright as a bundle of distinct rights, including the right to reproduce, to distribute, to prepare derivative works, to publicly perform or display, and so on. It also established that each component of that bundle can be transferred, licensed, retained, or encumbered independently. Rights transfer agreements are the instruments through which those transfers occur.

The critical distinction among the three agreements turns on whether the writer is transferring ownership of the right or only granting permission to exercise it. That distinction determines whether the counterparty acquires an asset they can sell, sublicense, or use indefinitely, or merely an authorization that expires, reverts, or remains subject to conditions the writer can enforce. It's similar to the difference between selling your house and renting it. Both transactions give the other party access to the property, but only one gives them title.

The Literary Purchase Agreement

A literary purchase agreement is the definitive acquisition instrument of the entertainment industry. It is the agreement by which a studio, network, streaming platform, or production company acquires the rights to a literary property, typically a screenplay, novel, article, life story, or other narrative work, for the purpose of producing a film, television series, or other audiovisual adaptation. When an option is exercised and the purchase price is paid, the instrument that governs that acquisition is in essence the literary purchase agreement. When a project is acquired without a preceding option, the literary purchase agreement is the first and only transactional document.

In structural terms, a literary purchase agreement is a conveyance. It transfers ownership of specified rights from the writer to the acquiring party. What makes it distinct from a bare assignment is its specificity and comprehensiveness. A well-drafted literary purchase agreement defines with precision which rights are transferred and which are reserved; what the writer is paid and on what schedule; what credit the writer is entitled to receive; what participation the writer has in revenues derived from the work; under what circumstances rights may revert to the writer; and what obligations the acquiring party assumes with respect to production, sequel and remake rights, and the writer's ongoing involvement in the project.

What Is Typically Acquired

The rights conveyed in a literary purchase agreement are typically broad and often described as "all motion picture rights," "all television rights," or, in many modern agreements, "all rights in all media now known or hereafter devised throughout the universe in perpetuity." That last version is a deliberate drafting choice by acquiring parties to cover all mediums as technology evolves in ways that contracts cannot anticipate, and to ensure that no subsequently developed medium or platform falls outside the scope of their acquisition.

The rights conveyed are the rights the writer will no longer have. A grant of "all rights" or even a grant that appears comprehensive but is poorly defined can strip a writer of the ability to write a novel sequel to her own screenplay, to authorize a stage adaptation of her own life story, or to develop a podcast based on the same underlying narrative. Every right that is transferred is a right that cannot be exploited by the writer without going back to the acquirer for consent or purchase.

This is why the reserved rights provision of a literary purchase agreement is often as important as the grant itself. Reserved rights are the rights the writer expressly retains and that are carved out from the scope of the acquisition. Common reservations include publication rights (the right to publish the underlying work as a book), stage rights (the right to authorize live theatrical adaptations), radio rights, podcast rights, merchandising, and interactive media rights. What is reserved in any given negotiation depends on the nature of the underlying work, the breadth of the acquirer's grant, and the writer's sophistication in identifying which rights carry independent commercial value.

The Purchase Price and Its Structure

The purchase price in a literary purchase agreement is typically structured in layers rather than paid as a single lump sum. There is usually a fixed purchase price paid upon execution of the agreement or upon exercise of a preceding option. There may be a milestone payment triggered upon the commencement of principal photography. The agreement may also provide for net or profit participation that entitles the writer to a percentage of defined revenues once the project reaches a negotiated breakeven threshold. And there may be separated rights payments, residuals, and other guild-mandated or contractually negotiated compensatory elements that are payable over time as the project moves through its commercial life.

Each of these layers, and the definitions governing them, is a point of negotiation. Deal points will be addressed in detail in the chapters that follow. But it is worth noting here that the relationship between the purchase price structure and the rights conveyance is not merely financial but also has legal consequences. A writer who is paid a purchase price in exchange for a broad rights grant has conveyed those rights permanently and irrevocably, regardless of whether the acquiring party ever produces the project. The reversion provisions of the agreement are the only mechanism by which a writer can recover rights that have been sold and paid for. Their absence, or their inadequacy, is among the most consequential deficiencies that can appear in a literary purchase agreement.

PRO TIP:

A purchase agreement without a reversion provision is a permanent transfer. The writer who signs it has transferred her rights with no legal path to recovery if the acquiring party does nothing with the project.

A writer will encounter a literary purchase agreement whenever a party with acquisition authority decides to formally acquire her work. That moment may follow the exercise of a long-negotiated option, or it may arrive without any preliminary option period in cases where the acquiring party's interest is immediate and the writer's leverage is sufficient to compel a direct acquisition offer. In either case, the literary purchase agreement is the end of the development phase and the beginning of the production relationship. What is agreed in that document will govern the writer's relationship with the project, if any, with the studio, and the acquirer for the full commercial life of the work.

The License

A license is a grant of permission to exercise one or more rights in a copyrighted work without a transfer of ownership of those rights. It authorizes another to use, distribute, perform, or otherwise exploit a work with the owner retaining the underlying ownership. The licensor is the party who grants the permission and remains the copyright owner. The licensee is the party who receives the permission and acquires the right to exercise the specified rights within the specified parameters, subject to the terms the licensor has negotiated and imposed.

The distinction between a license and an outright transfer is important to understand. A licensee does not own what it has been licensed to use. It cannot sell the rights it has been granted, sublicense them to a third party, or exercise them outside the scope, territory, duration, or conditions specified in the license unless the license agreement expressly permits those things. An assignee or purchaser, by contrast, typically acquires the rights as an owner and can use them accordingly. For a writer, the difference between licensing a right and selling it is the difference between a temporary arrangement that will come back and a permanent divestiture of rights.

Exclusive Versus Non-Exclusive Licenses

Licenses are granted on a spectrum of exclusivity that materially affects their value and their legal character. An exclusive license grants the licensee the right to exercise the licensed rights to the exclusion of everyone else, including the licensor herself. For example, a writer who grants an exclusive license to produce a television series based on her novel cannot simultaneously authorize a different production company to produce a competing television adaptation of the same work. The exclusivity eliminates that flexibility for the duration of the license.

A non-exclusive license, by contrast, grants the licensee the right to exercise the licensed rights while leaving the licensor free to grant the same rights to other parties simultaneously. Non-exclusive licenses are common in certain industries, such as music synchronization licensing or stock footage licensing, but they are rarely used in major film and television acquisitions. No serious production company will invest in developing a project if the underlying rights can be simultaneously licensed to a competitor.

A third category worth noting, though it arises less frequently in the entertainment context, is the sole license. A sole license is used in scenarios where the rightsholder needs to use the rights for their own exploitation and thus it is exclusive as between the licensor and the licensee but under which the licensor herself retains the right to exercise the licensed rights. Writers occasionally encounter this construct in non-production contexts, such as merchandise licensing or digital distribution agreements, where the distinction between the licensor's retained rights and the licensee's grant has practical commercial significance.

Duration, Territory, and Scope

Every license is defined, either expressly or by implication, by three parameters: duration, territory, and scope. Duration is the period for which the license is effective, which may be fixed (three years, ten years), tied to a defined event (the theatrical release of the film, the broadcast of the final episode), or perpetual. Territory defines the geographic markets in which the licensee may exercise the licensed rights, such as worldwide, North America, a specific country, or a defined set of jurisdictions. Scope defines what the licensee may actually do under the license: produce, distribute, broadcast, sublicense, stream, merchandise, or any specified combination thereof.

Each of these parameters is a negotiating point, and the interaction among them determines the practical value of what the writer is granting. A worldwide perpetual license with an unrestricted scope of exploitation is, for most commercial purposes, indistinguishable from an outright transfer particularly if the license does not include meaningful reversion or termination provisions. Conversely, a narrowly defined license with a fixed duration, a limited territory, and a carefully circumscribed scope of use gives the writer maximum retained control over how the work is used and where. Writers who are licensing rather than selling their work should understand to which of these arrangements they are actually agreeing.

Termination and Reversion

One of the most practically significant differences between a license and an outright assignment is that a license can be terminated. A license with a fixed duration terminates automatically at expiration.

A license conditioned on specified events terminates if those events do not occur. A license containing material breach provisions can be terminated if the licensee fails to meet its obligations. And under 17 U.S.C. § 203, authors retain a statutory right to terminate copyright grants, including licenses, made after January 1, 1978, during a five-year window beginning thirty-five years after the execution of the grant, subject to specific procedural requirements.

That termination right can be a valuable reserved right fallback that a writer possesses. It applies to grants of rights, not to works made for hire which are owned outright by the commissioning party from the moment of creation. Writers who structure their agreements as licenses rather than as assignments or work-for-hire arrangements preserve the statutory termination right as a future option, even if they never intend to exercise it.

Writers encounter license agreements most commonly in three contexts: the licensing of television and streaming rights in a work that the writer wishes to retain in other formats; the licensing of a specific right, such as translation, merchandise, or format rights, as a standalone transaction separate from the primary production agreement; and the licensing of work to a non-exclusive platform or aggregator where the writer retains the ability to simultaneously grant the same rights elsewhere. In each context, the key question is under what circumstances and on what timeline do these rights come back to you.

Book Publishing Contract

Although not termed as a license, a book publishing contract is essentially an exclusive license granting the publisher the right to publish the copyrighted work owned by the author. The author, who holds the copyright, is the licensor who grants the publisher, the licensee, an exclusive license to use the copyright to publish and distribute the book. While under contract, the author is disallowed to publish the book herself or with another publisher. Like any license deal, a book publishing contract can be short or last over years, if not decades, with the publishing rights and subsidiary rights being exploited and/or reverting back to the author ideally on her terms. The deal points that follow are the most important ones that can alter your book rights for years to come. Like any other rights acquisition agreement discussed, it is highly advised to have an experienced attorney negotiate these points on your behalf.

Grant of Rights

The grant clause defines the scope of what the author is licensing to the publisher and is the most consequential provision in the agreement. A narrow grant licenses only the rights the publisher actually intends to exploit, typically print and eBook rights in a defined territory and language. A broad license, on the other hand, grants the publisher "all rights worldwide and throughout the universe in all languages and in every medium now known or hereafter devised." The broader the grant, the more the author is licensing away in a single transaction, and the less she retains for separate negotiation with publishers, producers, or licensees who specialize in those individual markets. For most authors, the appropriate grant sits closer to the narrow end of that spectrum than to the broad end.

The territory and language should however be no broader than that which the publisher will publish. World English rights are appropriate for a publisher with genuine distribution in the United States, the United Kingdom, and the Commonwealth; for a publisher who only distributes in North America, the grant should be limited accordingly so the author can license the U.K. and Commonwealth markets separately. If there is a possibility that the publisher may have the ability to exploit certain subsidiary rights, then a negotiation to allow the publisher a specified amount of time to do so may be an agreed upon concession.

Subsidiary Rights (Including Film and Television)

As part of the rights granted, a typical publishing agreement contains a separate clause with its own royalty structure as it pertains to what's known as *subsidiary rights*. Subsidiary rights include rights such as audiobook, film and television, dramatic, merchandising, podcasting, foreign translation, and serial rights. For authors who aspire their book being on screen one day, this is the section that most applies.

The film and television rights in a published book are the bridge between the publishing world and the screen industry, and they are the reason book-to-screen adaptation has become one of the most active categories of acquisition in Hollywood. When a producer, studio, or streamer becomes interested in adapting a published book, they are not buying the book itself; they are acquiring the film and television rights that sit inside the larger bundle of subsidiary rights granted, or reserved, under the publishing agreement. Where those rights were retained by the author, the deal is negotiated directly between the author (typically through her literary agent or entertainment attorney) and the producer. Where those rights were granted to the publisher, the producer must deal with the publisher's subsidiary rights department, and the author's economic participation will be governed by the split set out in the publishing agreement, which is typically fifty-fifty between author and publisher on film and television proceeds, though this is negotiable.

The instrument by which film and television rights in a book are acquired is, almost without exception, an option or option purchase agreement of the kind discussed already. A producer who has read the book and wants to develop it as a film or limited series rarely has the resources or the certainty to buy the rights outright at the moment of first interest. Instead, she options the rights for a defined period (typically twelve to eighteen months, with one or more extensions) for a modest option payment, during which she attaches a screenwriter, develops a script, attaches talent, and seeks financing or a studio home. If the producer succeeds in setting the project up, she exercises the option and the negotiated purchase price is paid. If she does not, the rights revert to the author (or to the publisher, depending on who granted them) and the project can be optioned again to someone else.

The subsidiary rights are one of the most negotiated sections of a publishing contract. Unless the publisher has a film agent in-house or can demonstrate it has other infrastructure to exploit, then the author should reconsider granting the film, television, and dramatic rights, since those rights are most efficiently negotiated through a literary agent or entertainment attorney rather than by a publisher. The same logic applies to the other subsidiary rights, such as podcasting, audiobook, merchandising, and, yes, even theme park rights. Your book could be the next *Harry Potter*.

Advance and Royalties

The advance is a prepayment against royalties, paid in installments tied to defined milestones such as signing, delivery and acceptance of the manuscript, and publication. The advance is recoupable, meaning the publisher retains all royalties earned by the book until the advance has been paid back in full, after which the author begins receiving royalty payments. The advance is generally not refundable if the book underperforms, provided the author has delivered an acceptable manuscript.

Royalty rates vary by format and by whether the publisher is a major trade house or an independent press, but typical ranges include ten to fifteen percent of the hardcover list price, seven and a half percent to ten percent of the trade paperback list price, and twenty-five percent of the publisher's net receipts on eBooks and audiobooks. The author should pay close attention to whether royalties are calculated on list price (a fixed published price) or on net receipts (what the publisher actually collects after retailer discounts), since net-receipts royalties on heavily discounted sales can produce materially lower payments than the headline rate suggests. In most cases, the royalty will be calculated on the net, and unless the author has substantial leverage, the publisher is unlikely to agree to change their accounting method. That being said, it's important that the contract contains the definition of "net receipts" or "net profits" and that it doesn't include discretionary expenses, i.e. marketing, that would in effect swallow up any potential profits.

Manuscript Delivery and Acceptance

The agreement will specify a delivery date for the completed manuscript and will give the publisher the right to accept or reject the manuscript based on editorial quality. A rejection clause that allows the publisher to declare the manuscript unacceptable in its sole discretion gives the publisher unilateral power to terminate the deal and demand return of the advance, which is a significant risk for the author. The author should negotiate for an acceptance standard that is objective rather than discretionary, such as a requirement that the manuscript be "professionally competent and fit for publication," and for a meaningful opportunity to revise the manuscript in response to editorial notes before any rejection becomes final. The author should also negotiate to retain the portion of the advance already paid even if the agreement is ultimately terminated for non-acceptance, or at minimum to repay the advance only out of proceeds from a subsequent sale of the book to another publisher.

Publication Obligations and Out-of-Print Reversion

A publishing contract that does not obligate the publisher to actually publish the book within a defined period is a contract that allows the publisher to sit on the rights indefinitely. The agreement should require publication within twelve to eighteen months of acceptance of the manuscript, with the rights reverting automatically to the author if the publisher fails to publish by that date. Equally important is the out-of-print clause, which governs what happens when the book is no longer being actively sold. In the era of print-on-demand and eBooks, a publisher can technically keep a book "in print" indefinitely with negligible sales, which would tie up the rights forever under a traditional out-of-print definition. The author should negotiate for a sales-based reversion trigger on the paper copies, such as the right to terminate and recover the rights if royalties fall below a defined threshold over two consecutive accounting periods, regardless of whether the book is technically available for sale.

Option on Next Work

Most publishing contracts contain an option clause giving the publisher a first look, and sometimes a right of first refusal or matching right, on the author's next book. Option clauses vary widely in how restrictive they are. The author should resist any option that requires the next book to be submitted before the current book has been published, since the publisher's actual performance on the current book is the most important data point in deciding whether to offer the next one to the same house. The option should be limited to a single next work in the same genre, should require the publisher to make an offer within a short, defined period (thirty to sixty days), and should free the author to shop the work elsewhere if the publisher's offer is not matched by another publisher's offer.

Warranties, Representations, and Indemnification

The author will be required to warrant that the work is original, does not infringe any third-party copyright, does not defame any person, and does not violate any right of privacy or publicity. Some publishers are now including AI clauses in their publishing agreements to ensure the work wasn't created, or substantially created, by the author's use of AI. The reason this is important goes back to Chapter 1 of this book and that is the copyright. Work created by AI is not copyrightable.

A publisher is only interested in work that can be safeguarded by copyright law. Conversely, authors will want to ensure that their work isn't going to be knowingly used by the publisher for generative AI purposes.

The indemnification clause is what backs up the warranties clause and where the author's exposure is created. A broad indemnification obligates the author to defend and reimburse the publisher for any claim, even an unsuccessful one, arising from the warranties. The author should negotiate for the indemnification to be limited to claims that result in a final adverse judgment or a settlement to which the author has consented, should cap the author's financial exposure at the amounts received under the agreement, and should require the publisher to maintain media perils insurance covering the work, with the author named as an additional insured. Without these protections, an author can be on the hook for legal fees that exceed the entire advance and royalty stream the book ever generates.

PRO TIP:

A publishing contract should provide that the copyright is to be filed in the author's name—not the publisher's name. Otherwise, the contract is a rights transfer rather than a license and not consistent with industry standards.

The Assignment

An assignment is the outright transfer of one or more rights in a copyrighted work from one party to another. Where a license grants permission while retaining ownership, an assignment transfers ownership itself. The assignor steps out of the chain of title. The assignee steps in. After a valid copyright assignment, the assignor has no more ownership interest in the assigned right than a property seller has in a house she has conveyed by deed. The right belongs to the assignee, who may in turn assign it, license it, encumber it, or exploit it as the new owner sees fit, subject only to whatever restrictions the assignment agreement expressly imposes.

Under 17 U.S.C. § 204(a), a copyright assignment must be in writing and signed by the party conveying the rights. An oral agreement to assign a copyright regardless of the clarity of the parties' mutual intent, regardless of any reliance by the assignee, regardless of any consideration paid is unenforceable as an assignment. It is a statutory requirement that the assignment be in writing. For example, a production company that paid six figures for what both parties understood to be a copyright assignment, but failed to execute a written instrument, does not own the copyright. This is one of the most preventable chain of title defects in the industry.

The Assignment as a Term of Art

In entertainment transactions, the word "assignment" is used in two related but distinct senses that are worth separating. In the broader sense, any outright transfer of copyright, including the rights conveyed in a literary purchase agreement, is technically an assignment. The literary purchase agreement is, among other things, an assignment of the specified rights from the writer to the acquiring party, and its chain of title function depends on that assignment being properly executed and documented.

In the narrower, more transactional sense, however, an "assignment" often refers specifically to a short-form instrument in the form of a discrete document executed for the purpose of transferring a defined right from one party to another, without the elaborate deal-point structure of a full literary purchase agreement. This narrower instrument appears most commonly as a certificate of authorship executed by a writer to confirm that a work was created as a work made for hire and to assign all rights in the alternative; a quitclaim assignment executed by a party who may have a colorable claim to a copyright interest, relinquishing whatever claim they may hold; or a short-form assignment filed in the Copyright Office to create a public record of a rights transfer that was fully documented in a longer-form agreement not filed for public record.

Each of these instruments serves a distinct chain of title function, and each is governed by the same statutory requirement: (1) it must be in writing, (2) it must identify the rights being transferred with sufficient specificity to establish the scope of the conveyance, and (3) it must be signed by the party transferring the rights. The party receiving the rights does not need to sign an assignment for it to be effective, though it is often prudent to obtain signatures from all parties for evidentiary purposes.

The Permanence of the Assignment

The most important practical characteristic of an assignment is its permanence. An assignment, absent an express provision for reversion or a statutory termination right, is forever. The writer who assigns all rights in her screenplay to a production company for a fixed purchase price has, in the absence of any other protective mechanism, permanently divested herself of those rights. If the production company is acquired, the rights go with it. If the production company goes bankrupt, the rights become an asset of the estate. If the production company elects to put the project in turnaround and never produce it, the rights remain with the production company, unless the agreement contains a reversion clause that triggers upon non-production. The beauty and the beast of an assignment is its simultaneous simplicity and permanence.

PRO TIP:

An assignment without a reversion provision is a permanent transfer of rights.

Hence, this is precisely why the distinction between a license and an assignment matters in practical terms for every writer who is not receiving an unconditional payment that adequately compensates for permanent divestiture. A license that expires, reverts, or can be terminated is a fundamentally different commercial arrangement from an assignment that transfers title permanently. Writers who understand that distinction are in a position to negotiate accordingly, insisting on license structures where the permanence of an assignment is not warranted by the consideration being paid, and accepting assignments where the purchase price and protective deal terms are sufficient to justify the transfer of ownership.

Work Made for Hire and the Assignment Alternative

A similar agreement to the assignment is a work-made-for-hire agreement. Under 17 U.S.C. § 101, a work is a work made for hire if it is created by an employee within the scope of employment, or in the case of certain categories of commissioned works if it is created pursuant to a written agreement that expressly designates it as a work made for hire. For screenplays created under commission agreements, studios and production companies frequently characterize the writer's services as work for hire, which means the studio, not the writer, is the legal author of the work from the moment of creation.

The work-for-hire characterization has significant implications for the assignment analysis, because copyright in a work made for hire cannot be terminated under § 203. There is no thirty-five-year termination window for a statutory reversion right. The commissioning party owns the copyright permanently, as a matter of law, without any assignment being required. This is why entertainment attorneys drafting commissioning agreements on behalf of studios include both the work-for-hire characterization and an alternative assignment provision usually stating that if the work-for-hire characterization is challenged or does not hold up for some reason, the assignment operates as a fallback to ensure that the rights transfer is effective regardless. Writers signing commissioning agreements should understand that this belt-and-suspenders drafting approach is standard and should negotiate accordingly for the deal terms that provide meaningful protection in a work-for-hire context, where the statutory termination right will not be available.

Assignments typically arise in the entertainment space involving the following scenarios: (1) at the closing of a literary purchase agreement when the operative provisions effect a copyright transfer from writer to acquirer, (2) in connection with commissioning agreements where the writer is being hired to create a new work and the studio wishes to own the result, (3) in chain of title cleanup where a defective or missing transfer instrument needs to be remedied or supplemented, and (4) in co-authorship situations where one co-author assigns her interest to a third party or to the other co-author.

In each context, the writer should understand that what is being signed is a transfer of ownership and not a permission or a temporary authorization, but a conveyance. In such cases, it's important to ensure that the consideration and protective provisions of the surrounding agreement are commensurate with what is being permanently given away.

The following comparison is for reference. The specific terms of any executed agreement govern.

Feature	**Literary Purchase Agreement**	**License**	**Assignment**
Ownership Transfer?	Yes — specified rights conveyed to acquirer	No — licensor retains ownership	Yes — full ownership transferred

Feature	Literary Purchase Agreement	License	Assignment
Duration	Perpetual unless reversion triggered	Fixed, conditional, or perpetual	Permanent unless expressly limited
Reversion Possible?	Yes, via negotiated reversion clause	Yes, at expiration or termination	Only if expressly provided
Statutory Termination?	Yes (§ 203), unless work for hire	Yes (§ 203), unless work for hire	Yes (§ 203), unless work for hire
Writer Retains Copyright?	No, as to rights conveyed	Yes	No, as to rights assigned
Must Be in Writing?	Yes (§ 204(a))	Exclusive licenses: yes. Non-exclusive: technically no, but advisable	Yes (§ 204(a))
Typical Context	Studio/ platform acquisition of produced or optioned work	Television, streaming, format, or limited-use grants	Commissioning, chain of title cleanup, co-author buyouts

The Stakes of Getting It Right

The agreements covered in this chapter occupy the top of the risk hierarchy in entertainment and publishing transactions. They are the documents that determine whether, at the end of a deal, the writer retains a meaningful connection to her work or has permanently divested herself of it in exchange for a payment that, however substantial it seemed at signing, may bear no relationship to the work's ultimate commercial value.

Writers sometimes treat the choice among these instruments as a formality as though the deal points that will be negotiated in subsequent chapters are the substance of the transaction and the instrument itself is merely the vessel. However, the choice of conveyance determines the legal structure of the entire relationship. A license with robust reversion provisions is fundamentally different from an assignment, even if both documents specify the same purchase price and the same credit entitlement. The deal points are only as meaningful as the legal structure that makes them enforceable and the legal structure is determined by the instrument. That being said, it's important to reiterate that one should never assume that the title of the document is a correct descriptor of the effect of its provisions.

The chapters that follow will examine the major deal points in detail: the price, the term, the credit, the backend, the reversion. In every case, those points should be understood against the background of this chapter as provisions that operate within the framework of one of these three instruments, and whose practical significance depends on which framework is in place. A reversion clause in a literary purchase agreement is doing something different than a termination clause in a license. A backend participation in an assignment is legally different from one in a work-for-hire commissioning agreement. As we get into the details of the agreement, it's crucial to keep the bigger picture of what's being conveyed in mind.

CHAPTER 11

STORY RIGHTS

This chapter is about what story rights actually are, how they differ from the rights instruments covered in preceding chapters, when you need them, and what the agreement looks like when you do. In practice, the terms "story rights" and "life rights" are often used interchangeably in the industry, and you will hear them deployed almost as synonyms in development meetings, option agreements, and trade press coverage. That conflation is understandable. Both involve the acquisition of rights from a real person subject whose experiences, identity, or circumstances form the basis of a proposed audiovisual project. But the distinction is worth discussing because it has meaningful consequences for what the producer obtains and what the writer is actually licensed to portray.

The difference lies in *scope*. Life rights, strictly construed, refer to the comprehensive acquisition of rights associated with a person's life as a whole. In other words, it is the right to portray the subject's identity, biography, name, likeness, personal history, and the arc of their experiences across time, together with the subject's cooperation, waivers of defamation and right-of-publicity claims, and, where available, access to personal materials such as letters, photographs, and journals. A life rights agreement is, in effect, a license to dramatize the person using content that expands most, if not all, of the subject's life.

Story rights, by contrast, are narrower and event specific. A story rights agreement grants the producer the right to dramatize a particular incident, episode, or defined chapter in the subject's life, i.e. the heist, the trial, the rescue, the scandal, without conveying broader rights to portray the subject's identity or biography beyond the four corners of that specific story. A survivor of a widely reported disaster may grant story rights to the events of a single day while retaining the right to license a full biographical treatment separately. A convicted defendant may grant story rights to the criminal case while retaining rights to his broader life narrative.

Ultimately, the agreement you negotiate should match the project you are making. A producer developing a limited series about a public figure's career arc needs life rights; a story rights agreement will leave material gaps in what the production is licensed to depict. A producer developing a feature about a single confined event needs story rights; a full life rights deal is broader and therefore more expensive than the project requires. As with every other instrument discussed in this book, the label on the agreement does not control. What controls is the operative language defining the scope of what is being conveyed, not the title of the document. For convenience, the terms life rights and story rights will be used interchangeably throughout this chapter.

What Are Story Rights

A story rights agreement is a contract between a producer (or writer, or studio) and a real person or the subject whose life, experiences, or story the production intends to depict granting permission to use that person's personal story as the basis for a film, television series, book, or other dramatic work. This is what practitioners usually mean when they talk about getting someone's story rights or life rights.

In broader usage, story rights sometimes refers to any agreement that secures the right to use source material that is not itself a literary property subject to copyright. The rights at issue in these deals are not copyright rights in the conventional sense. Instead, they are something more nuanced: a bundle of personal, privacy, and reputational rights that real people hold in their own stories. These rights are distinct from, but often intersect with, the intellectual property rights in written accounts of those stories.

The distinction is consequential because it determines which rights you need to clear and from whom. A screenwriter who adapts a published memoir is dealing with copyright as we've previously discussed and needs a license or option from the publisher or the author-copyright holder. However, a screenwriter who dramatizes the events described in that memoir, including conversations, private moments, and personal details that the subject did not publish, may be dealing with something different: the living person's rights to control how their life story is used for commercial purposes. These are not always the same rights, held by the same party, governed by the same legal framework.

Some writers or producers believe that life rights are always required whenever a real person is depicted in a film or television project. Others believe that, because there is no legally codified right called life rights, the concept is merely a courtesy and something nice to have but not legally essential. The truth lies somewhere in the middle.

There is no single federal statute governing one's right to life story. What we refer to as story rights or life rights is, in practice, a shorthand for several distinct legal rights that real people hold under state law. To make the matter more confusing, the rights vary in scope and enforceability depending on the state jurisdiction. There have been recent legislative efforts to codify these rights into federal law to bring cohesion across state lines. However, taken together, *privacy rights* give a living person meaningful legal grounds to object to the unauthorized commercial use of their personal narrative. The principal rights implicated vary by state but generally include the following:

Right of Publicity

The right to control the commercial use of one's name, likeness, voice, and, in many states, other identifying characteristics. California Civil Code § 3344 and similar statutes in other states provide statutory causes of action for unauthorized commercial use. The right of publicity survives death in many jurisdictions for a defined period. California extends it seventy years post-mortem for personalities whose identity retains commercial value.

Right of Privacy

The common law and, in some states, statutory right to be free from unauthorized public disclosure of private facts. A dramatization that depicts real events, real conversations, and real private moments that were never publicly disclosed implicates this right, regardless of whether the depiction is accurate.

Defamation

A dramatized account that depicts a living person in a false and damaging light creates potential defamation liability. This can include a fictional composite or a dramatic embellishment that the production characterizes as 'based on a true story.' A signed life rights agreement typically includes a release of defamation claims and a warranty of cooperation, both of which significantly reduce the production's legal exposure.

False Light Claims

Distinct from defamation, false light is an invasion of privacy tort that attaches when a person is depicted in a manner that, even if not technically false, places them in a false or objectionable light before the public. A docudrama that puts words in a real person's mouth or attributes motivations to them that they dispute can give rise to false light liability even if no specific statement of fact is incorrect.

A life rights agreement when properly drafted addresses all of these exposures simultaneously. And that is ultimately the reason to have a legal agreement that secures consent, grants authorization, limits the subject's future claims against the production, and provides the cooperation and access that make a biographical or true-story project viable as a commercial project.

When Do You Actually Need Life Rights?

The operative question is not whether a real person is depicted in your project. Real people appear in all manner of films and television series without triggering any obligation to secure their life rights. The question is whether the nature of your depiction, and the commercial context in which it will appear, creates the kind of legal exposure that a life rights agreement is designed to address. The following factors bear on this analysis.

Living Versus Deceased Subjects

Life rights concerns are most acute with living subjects. A deceased person cannot be defamed under most state laws, cannot bring a privacy claim, and holds no personal right of publicity (though post-mortem publicity rights may vest in the estate, as discussed below). Historical figures who have been dead for decades present an essentially different risk profile from living persons who are capable of asserting claims, granting or withholding cooperation, and making the production's life difficult in practical as well as legal terms.

Public Figures Versus Private Individuals

Public figures, including politicians, executives, celebrities, prominent athletes, have voluntarily entered public life and, under the First Amendment framework established in *New York Times Co. v. Sullivan* and its progeny, accept a higher degree of public scrutiny and have diminished privacy interests in their public conduct. Documentaries, dramatizations, and satires of public figures are constitutionally protected expression in ways that similar depictions of private individuals are not. This does not eliminate the need for life rights in every case involving a public figure, but it does shift the risk calculus significantly.

Private Facts and Dramatic Fabrication

The more your project depicts private moments, private conversations, internal emotional states, or events that were never part of the public record the more significant your exposure and the more important a life rights agreement becomes. Add to that, situations where dramatization embellishes, speculates, or invents those private events, such as a docudrama that reconstructs actual conversations no one witnessed, attributes thoughts and motivations to real people, or dramatizes bedroom scenes and private confrontations. This becomes something categorically different from a documentary that draws exclusively on the public record.

> **PRO TIP:**
>
> Memoirists are often most concerned about getting the truth correct to avoid defamation, however the more likely landmine is private facts in which private persons hold certain privacy rights.

The Cooperation Premium

Even when a project might be legally defensible without a life rights agreement, the practical value of the subject's cooperation is often decisive. A subject who cooperates provides access to personal archives, introduces the production to other participants, participates in interviews, and vouches for the project's authenticity. A subject who does not cooperate may speak publicly against the project, decline to participate in promotional activities, and, if the project makes any legally exploitable misstep, sue. The risk-adjusted value of securing cooperation is usually substantial.

Public Record is Not a Safe Harbor

Writers frequently assume that, because information appeared in a newspaper article or court record, it is freely usable in a dramatization without any obligation to the subject. This is partially but not entirely correct. Public records protect you against defamation claims based on accurately reported facts. They do not protect you against right-of-publicity claims, false light claims arising from dramatic embellishment, or privacy claims based on your use of information that was technically public but that the subject never authorized for dramatic commercial use. If your project will be sold, licensed, or commercially distributed, 'it was in the newspaper' is not a complete answer to any of these claims. Not to mention potential copyright infringement issues discussed in previous chapters.

When Story Rights Overlap with Copyrights

Having clarified what story rights are and when they matter, it is worth distinguishing them from the other rights agreements with overlapping concerns. An option or literary purchase agreement involves a copyright-protected written work, such as a novel, memoir, screenplay, or article, that is being acquired for the right to adapt into a film or television project. However, the subject of the adaptation may be real. The rights being acquired are property rights in a written work, not personal rights held by a living human being.

A life rights agreement involves personal rights, meaning the right of a living person to consent to the commercial dramatization of their life, experiences, and story. There may be no copyrighted written work at all. In fact, the rights may likely be from someone who has never published anything, i.e. a crime victim, a whistleblower, a survivor, a private individual who happened to be at the center of a significant event. The rights at issue are that person's publicity rights, privacy rights, and defamation-related claims and not ownership of any written property.

The two categories often overlap when the subject has written a memoir. In that case, you may need both the copyright license or option from the publisher (or author as copyright holder) and a separate life rights agreement from the living author-subject. The memoir copyright gives you the right to adapt the text, but the author's personal rights in her own story exist independently of that copyright. Studios routinely require both rights. Relying solely on a memoir license without a life rights agreement leaves the production exposed to exactly the personal-rights claims the license does not address.

It is not uncommon to see a life rights provision tucked away in an option purchase agreement. This bypasses the need for two separate agreements and thus saves on legal fees. However, it's important that it is drafted and/or negotiated by an experienced entertainment attorney because the life rights agreement contains ancillary provisions that are not included short of a fully drafted agreement with the provisions contained below.

PRO TIP:

The cost of life rights, and the leverage the subject holds, increases in direct proportion to the producer's sunk costs. Address story rights at the earliest possible stage of any project involving a real, living person whose cooperation or consent is material.

What a Story Rights Agreement Looks Like

Because the parties and the subject matter differ fundamentally from those in a copyright option or purchase agreement, the deal points also differ. In fact, the document reads less like a property transaction and more like a consent, release, and collaboration agreement.

Grant of Rights

One of the core provisions in a life rights agreement is the grant of rights. The subject grants the producer (and by extension the studio, financier, and distribution chain) the right to use their name, likeness, biographical information, personal story, and life experiences in connection with the development, production, and exploitation of the project. The grant is typically exclusive (preventing the subject from granting the same rights to a competing project during the agreement term) and covers all media, territories, and formats. It should expressly include the producer's right to fictionalize, composite, and dramatize.

Release of Claims

Another essential element of the agreement is that the subject releases the production company, its successors, assignees, and licensees from all claims arising from the authorized use of their story, including claims for invasion of privacy, false light, defamation, and right of publicity. The release should be broad and survive the subject's later change of heart. A subject who cooperates enthusiastically during development and then sues after the film is released is not a hypothetical risk; it is a pattern that has occurred often enough to warrant robust release language as a non-negotiable provision.

Cooperation Obligations

Most life rights agreements include cooperation obligations, such as the subject will participate in a specified number of interviews, provide access to personal documents and photographs, make reasonable efforts to introduce the production to other participants in the events depicted, and generally cooperate in good faith with the production's research and development efforts. These obligations are valuable precisely because their value is difficult to capture after the fact. A cooperation agreement signed before production begins is worth considerably more than a cooperation promise made verbally after the subject has seen the director's cut.

Approval Rights

Subjects often request, short of demand, the right to approve the script, the casting, and the finished film. However, producers rarely give in. Approval rights are the most contentious deal point in life rights negotiations precisely because they go to the heart of the creative control question. A studio that grants a subject script approval has, in practice, given that subject veto power over the dramatization. The industry standard compromise is consultation rights without approval meaning that the production will consult with the subject on the script and casting and give good-faith consideration to the subject's concerns, but the final creative decisions remain with the producer and studio.

Compensation

Life rights compensation varies enormously with the commercial prominence of the subject and the competitive landscape at the time of negotiation. In straightforward cases involving private individuals, compensation may be a modest payment against a purchase price that triggers only if the project moves into production. In cases involving high-profile subjects whose cooperation is essential and whose story is being actively pursued by multiple producers, compensation can be substantial. Unlike a literary purchase, where price is typically benchmarked against guild minimums and market rates for comparable properties, life rights compensation has no fixed reference point and is largely a function of negotiating leverage.

Option and Reversion Structure

Like literary options, most life rights agreements are structured as options wherein the producer pays an upfront fee for an exclusive option period during which she may develop the project and, if development succeeds, exercise the option to purchase the rights for an agreed purchase price. Option periods and extension mechanics mirror those in literary option agreements. Reversion is equally important in the event the producer fails to exercise the option, or if the project dies in development. The subject's rights should revert cleanly so that the subject is not permanently tied to a project that never materialized.

Do You Always Need the Subject's Life Rights?

One of the most common misconceptions among writers developing projects based on real people is that a life rights agreement is a legal prerequisite. There is no statute, no judicial doctrine, and no constitutional provision that requires someone to obtain a subject's permission before telling a story about that person's life. The First Amendment protects a substantial body of expressive work that portrays real individuals without their consent, and the entertainment industry has relied on that protection for as long as it has existed. The question, then, is not whether life rights are legally required but whether acquiring them is practically advisable for the particular project at hand.

The clearest category of projects that do not require life rights involves public figures and matters of public concern. Historical biopics are the most common example. A film about Abraham Lincoln, Winston Churchill, or Alexander Hamilton does not require permission from the subject's estate. The lives of public figures, particularly those whose significance is historical rather than private, are legitimate subjects of public discourse and artistic treatment. Think *Lincoln*, *The Crown*, *Hamilton*, *Oppenheimer*, *Ford v Ferrari*, *The Social*

Network, *Vice*. None of these projects rested on a comprehensive life rights acquisition from the primary subjects or their estates, and none of them needed to. The underlying factual material was drawn from public records, published accounts, and historical scholarship. A dramatization or documentary-style production of public figures acting in their public capacities is squarely within the zone of First Amendment-protected expression.

The same principle extends to contemporary public figures with respect to their public conduct. A film dramatizing a sitting politician's legislative record, a technology executive's founding of a public company, or a celebrity's professional career does not require that person's consent. The right of publicity, which protects the commercial use of a person's name and likeness, contains well-established exceptions for news, commentary, biography, and expressive works. Defamation law requires falsity, and courts applying the *Sullivan* standard require public figures to demonstrate actual malice, which is a high standard that well-researched productions portraying public conduct accurately are generally able to withstand. A producer who waits for every public figure's blessing before telling their story will not make many films.

True crime is the other substantial category in which life rights are frequently unnecessary. Criminal proceedings are matters of public record. The facts established at trial, the evidence admitted into the record, the testimony of witnesses, and the reporting of contemporaneous news media are all available without consent from the defendant, the victims, or the investigators. *Zodiac*, *All the President's Men*, *Spotlight*, *American Crime Story: The People v. O.J. Simpson*, and a long list of true-crime limited series have proceeded based on trial transcripts, court filings, journalistic accounts, and published books—not life rights deals with the principals. Where a true-crime project draws on a specific published work, the relevant clearance is with the author and publisher of that work, not with the criminal defendant or the victims' families. A properly executed option or purchase agreement with a journalist who covered the case, combined with disciplined reliance on the public record, can support a production that would be substantially more expensive and more editorially constrained if it depended on life rights from the subjects themselves.

This does not mean life rights are never useful in these contexts as they often are for reasons that have less to do with legal necessity than with practical advantage. Subject cooperation yields access to personal materials, previously undisclosed details, private correspondence, and the emotional texture that comes only from sustained engagement with the person whose story is being told. A life rights deal also provides contractual waivers of defamation and right-of-publicity claims, which, while not legally required, meaningfully reduce litigation risk and simplify the errors-and-omissions insurance process. And in projects involving living subjects who retain significant public goodwill, an authorized treatment may enjoy marketing advantages, press cooperation, access to the subject for publicity, and the perception of authenticity that an unauthorized treatment cannot. In exchange, the person may negotiate payment for their cooperation or even inclusion in the production as is often the case with a documentary feature or docuseries.

The underlying principle is that a life rights agreement is a means of acquiring access, cooperation, waivers, and rights of publicity that the producer may need for a specific project. Where those things are not needed, or where they are available through other means, the agreement is not required. Understanding the difference helps a writer avoid proceeding without life rights where they are genuinely necessary and, on the contrary, spending substantial money and time acquiring life rights that are not needed.

Life Rights for Deceased Subjects

When the central subject of your project is deceased, the analysis shifts. The extent to which a deceased person's story is legally protectable depends on two factors: how recently they died, and whether they had the kind of fame and commercial identity that generates post-mortem publicity rights.

As noted above, California and several other states recognize post-mortem rights of publicity that survive death for a defined period. In California, rights of publicity survive death for seventy years for deceased personalities whose name or likeness has commercial value at the time of death. If you are making a dramatized film about a deceased celebrity, musician, athlete, or public figure who died within the last several decades, the estate may hold legally enforceable rights in the name and likeness, and failing to secure the estate's cooperation and consent can expose the production to claims that survived the subject's death. Estate-based right-of-publicity litigation is well-established, and estates are often far more litigious than living subjects.

For historical figures who have been dead for many decades and whose post-mortem publicity rights, if they ever existed, have expired, then the legal obligation to secure life rights largely dissolves. There is no living person to defame, no active privacy interest to protect, and no commercially enforceable right of publicity. That being said, descendants may object, historians may challenge accuracy, and the production may face criticism for its portrayal of a historical figure. But these are not generally legal risks of the kind that life rights agreements are designed to address.

Other Underlying Rights Deals Not Yet Discussed

Life rights and story rights agreements do not exhaust the category of underlying rights deals that a writer or producer may encounter. There are several additional instruments, less commonly discussed but no less legally significant, that bear on particular kinds of projects. Each represents a distinct rights question that should be addressed before development proceeds.

Format Rights

A *format* is the protectable concept, structure, and distinctive elements of a television program, particularly an unscripted or reality series. Format rights are the mechanism by which the creator of a television format licenses another producer or broadcaster to produce a version of that format in a different territory. Think of the global licensing apparatus behind shows like *The Voice*, *Big Brother*, or *Survivor*. Each local version is produced under a format license from the original creator, who retains ownership of the underlying format and receives royalties from every licensed production.

Format rights occupy an awkward position in copyright law because raw ideas are not protectable under 17 U.S.C. § 102(b), only the tangible expression of an idea is. Courts have been reluctant to extend robust copyright protection to television formats as abstract concepts, though the expression of a format in detailed written documents, show bibles, pilot scripts, and production materials can be protected. Format deals are therefore contractual rather than purely based in copyright law. The format license is the operative instrument, and its terms govern the licensee's right to produce local versions, the territory and duration of that license, the royalty and fee structure, and the extent to which the licensee must adhere to the original format's structure and distinctive elements.

For writers pitching unscripted or reality concepts, format rights are the relevant ownership category. Registering and documenting your format concept in a detailed written treatment or show bible is the best available protection and understanding that format deals are licensed rather than sold is essential to negotiating them intelligently.

Music Rights

Every time a piece of recorded music plays in a film or television episode, whether in the score, in a montage, under a scene, or as source music playing from a radio in the background, two separate licenses are required. Writers often do not encounter these agreements directly; they are typically negotiated by the production company, music supervisor, and business affairs team. But a writer whose work has reached production should understand them.

The synchronization license is obtained from the music publisher and grants the right to use the musical composition, which includes the melody and lyrics, synchronized to the picture. It is the license to use the song in the production. *The master use license* is obtained from the record label (or, increasingly, from an independent artist who owns their own masters) and grants the right to use the specific recorded performance, that is, the actual recording that plays in the film. For example, a project that wants to use Taylor Swift's recorded version of a song, rather than a cover version, needs a master use license from whatever entity owns that specific master recording.

The practical relevance for writers is if your script calls for a specific iconic song in a specific scene, then understand that clearing that music may be expensive, may be refused, or may not be available at any price. Productions regularly substitute different music when their first-choice song is unavailable or prohibitively expensive. Writing a script in which a specific song is structurally essential is a creative choice that comes with a downstream rights question. The same is true with using song lyrics in a book. A license to print all or any portion of the lyrics of a song should be obtained to avoid copyright infringement. Thus, the author's creative choice can come with extra expenses if unaware of the implications.

PRO TIP:

Refer to the song's title instead of the lyrics when referencing a particular song in a book. Titles are not copyrightable.

Location and Archive Rights

Documentaries, docudramas, and reality productions frequently need rights to use archival footage owned by third parties, rights to incorporate historical photographs, rights to reproduce news clips, and in some cases rights to use specific locations in ways that implicate the location owner's rights. These are distinct rights clearances that are separate from life rights or literary rights.

Archival footage is owned by the entity that holds the copyright in the recorded material, which is typically a news organization, a stock footage library, or a studio. Using archival news footage in a documentary or a book requires a license from the owner of that footage. Using a historical photograph requires a license from the copyright holder in the photograph (which may be the photographer, the publication that first ran it, or a stock agency). These licenses are usually transactional rather than complex, but the cost can be significant for high-demand archival materials, and some materials are simply unavailable at any price because the rights holder declines to license.

News and Podcast Adaptation Rights

One of the most active areas of rights acquisition in recent years has been the adaptation of podcast series, investigative journalism, and long-form magazine articles into dramatic films and television series. Each of these raises distinct rights questions that combine elements of literary rights and story rights in ways that are not always intuitive.

A podcast is, at its core, a copyright of an audio recording of speech. The podcast creator holds copyright in the recorded audio and in the expressive elements of the podcast's narration, structure, and presentation. But for the real people whose stories are told, they hold their own personal rights. In the instance with live guests, such as experts, the creator typically has the guest sign a release of their rights and to the resulting copyright of the show allowing the creator to distribute and exploit the episode as they want. This was the case for me as I guested on the *Law and Crime* podcast giving legal commentary on the *Depp v. Heard* trial. By virtue of the release I signed, the podcast could do what they wanted with the recording. As it happened, Netflix picked up a clip of the podcast to use in their documentary *Depp v. Heard*. Netflix most likely did not seek permission from *Law and Crime* and instead relied on fair use to use clips from the podcast episode.

For purposes of adapting a podcast into a dramatic series, it typically requires both a license from the podcast creator (or their publisher, if the podcast is affiliated with a media company) and a separate assessment of whether the real-person subjects depicted in the podcast require life rights clearances for the dramatic adaptation.

Investigative journalism adaptations present the same dual-track question. The newspaper or magazine holds copyright in the article as a work of authorship. The reporter who wrote it may hold a separate interest, depending on the terms of their employment. And the real subjects of the investigation, particularly those whose private conduct, private communications, or private lives are depicted, retain personal rights that the publication license does not address. A production that licenses a celebrated investigative article and dramatizes its contents without assessing the underlying subjects' rights is missing a significant piece of the underlying rights picture.

Rights in Formats Based on Games, IP, and Other Media

Films and television series are increasingly adapted from video games, comic books, graphic novels, board games, toys, and other media properties each of which presents its own rights clearance mandates. These adaptations typically involve copyright licenses from the IP owner (the game developer, comic publisher, or property owner), combined with trademark clearances for the title and distinctive elements, and in many cases with talent agreements for creative personnel whose involvement is part of the adaptation deal. It's no wonder that companies such as Mattel have their own in-house production arm in order to exploit their own IP.

The through line with all these adaptations that connects them to every other category of underlying rights discussed in this book is that you must trace the rights you need back to the person or entity that actually owns them. A video game publisher that licenses you the right to adapt a game may not control all of the underlying IP. The game may include licensed music, licensed character likenesses, or character designs that were themselves licensed from a comic book or film property. The adaptation license is only as good as the rights the licensor actually holds, and the due diligence obligation to verify that your licensor controls what they are purporting to convey.

Instrument	**What It Covers**	**Rights Acquired From**	**When Required**	**Key Risk If Absent**
Life Rights Agreement	Personal story, name, likeness, privacy, publicity rights of a living person	The living subject directly	Dramatization of real living person's private life or story	Privacy, false light, defamation, publicity rights claims
Estate Agreement (Post-Mortem)	Post-mortem publicity rights; cooperation of estate	Executor or estate of deceased subject	Deceased subject with commercial value within ~70 years	Right of publicity claims; estate opposition
Literary Option/ Purchase (Memoir)	Copyright in the written work (the book)	Author or publisher as copyright holder	Adapting a published memoir or autobiography	Copyright infringement by the author or estate

Instrument	What It Covers	Rights Acquired From	When Required	Key Risk If Absent
Format License	Right to produce a local version of a television format	Original format creator or rights holder	Producing a version of an existing format in a new territory	Format infringement; contractual breach; inability to distribute
Synchronization License	Right to use musical composition synchronized to picture	Music publisher	Any filmed use of a copyrighted song	Copyright infringement; takedowns; damages
Master Use License	Right to use specific recorded performance in a film	Record label or artist owning the master	Use of a specific recording (not a cover version)	Copyright infringement in the sound recording
Archival Footage/ Photo License	Right to reproduce third-party footage or photographs in a production	News organization, stock library, photographer, or studio	Documentary or docudrama use of historical footage or images	Copyright infringement; inability to clear E&O insurance

You now understand that before you can tell someone else's story commercially, you need the legal authority to do so, and that authority must come from the person or entity that holds the relevant rights. This sounds obvious, but it is often ignored out of excitement of a compelling story. Writers and producers fall in love with a subject, begin development, spend money, generate interest, and then discover that the legal foundation for the project has not been built. This can lead to the loss of development expenditures that were entirely preventable, and, in worst cases, litigation that poisons the entire project.

With the major categories of underlying rights instruments now covered, the chapters that follow break down the economic terms that will define what those rights are worth—the price, term, backend participation, credit provisions, and reversion mechanics.

ACT V

NEGOTIATING THE DEAL

The film was made and released. It performed well with a limited theatrical run followed by a streaming deal, strong reviews, and a festival award. By the time Cecilia's agent called to ask about her backend participation, the film had been generating revenue for fourteen months.

The answer, when it came, was zero.

Not because the film had lost money. Not because there had been any fraud or misrepresentation. But because Cecilia had sold her screenplay for a low flat fee with a larger backend profit participation. However, the provision was tied to "net proceeds as defined in the applicable distribution agreement," and the applicable distribution agreement defined net proceeds in a way that ensured, through a waterfall of permissible deductions, that net proceeds would not exist until the film had generated several multiples of its production budget after accounting for distribution fees, overhead allocations, interest charges, and marketing expenses that had been capitalized and then amortized over a period of years.

The purchase agreement Cecilia had signed was not fraudulent. It was entirely enforceable. The backend provision was real, in the sense that it had been written down and executed by both parties. It was simply structured in a way that made payment contingent on an outcome that the economics of independent film distribution make nearly impossible to achieve.

Her attorney, reviewing the agreement after the fact, found the definition in paragraph 14(c) of an exhibit that had been attached to a side letter. It was forty-seven words long and had cost Cecilia a meaningful portion of her participation in a film she had written.

CHAPTER 12

THE MAJOR DEAL POINTS

The preceding chapters covered what rights are, who owns them, and which agreements transfer those rights. Now let's turn to the deal points to determine whether the specific deal on the table is a fair one. Every agreement discussed in this book, regardless of its form or the rights it transfers, is ultimately defined by five main deal points: exclusivity, term, price, backend participation, and credit. These are the terms that lawyers negotiate most aggressively, that studios draft most carefully in their own favor, and that writers often accept without fully understanding what they have agreed to.

The goal of this chapter is to give you a working command of each deal point, not merely its definition, but its practical implications, its common formulations, and the red flags that signal a provision drafted against your interests. These terms appear in shopping agreements, option agreements, purchase agreements, life rights deals, and underlying rights licenses alike. The specific application varies by context, and where a particular agreement type presents a meaningfully different version of the analysis, that distinction is noted, but otherwise the framework is universal.

Exclusivity

Exclusivity is the provision that prevents you from doing something else with the material, by you or a third party, while the agreement is in effect. It is one of the most commercially significant provisions in any entertainment agreement. Like every other deal point, it's also negotiable. Exclusivity can be total or partial, broad or narrowly drawn, and the difference between these formulations has real consequences for a writer whose work may attract interest from multiple buyers simultaneously.

In the context of options, shopping agreements, literary purchase agreements, and life rights deals, exclusivity operates on the material. When a producer holds an exclusive option, you cannot option or sell those same rights to anyone else during the option period. You cannot shop the project independently. You cannot engage another producer. The rights are, for the term of the agreement, locked to that one party. This is the commercial bargain that justifies the option payment the producer pays for the exclusive right to develop the project without fear that the underlying material will be sold out from under them.

Exclusivity in a service context is when you are hired as a writer and operates on your time and labor. An exclusive writing engagement means that for the duration of that engagement, you work on that project and, to whatever extent the exclusivity provision specifies, nothing else. Broad exclusivity provisions in writing agreements can prevent you from developing your own projects, moonlighting on other assignments, or even writing on spec during the engagement period.

What Exclusivity Clauses Actually Say

Exclusivity provisions are rarely labeled 'Exclusivity' in a contract. They are more commonly embedded in the rights grant: "Producer shall have the exclusive right to develop, produce, and exploit the Work." The exclusivity provision provides what is permitted with respect to the rights, during what period, and in what territory.

Exclusivity can be worldwide or limited to specific markets. A shopping agreement that grants a producer the exclusive right to pitch the project in the United States and Canada, but leaves you free to pursue international co-productions independently, is a meaningfully different deal from one that locks the rights globally. Studios prefer global exclusivity as a matter of course. A writer with a genuinely commercial international property with obvious appeal in European or Asian markets has a legitimate basis to negotiate a narrower territorial scope, or at minimum to insist on a higher payment in exchange for global exclusivity.

Partial Exclusivity and Reserved Rights

Option agreements commonly grant exclusivity in all media including film, television, streaming, theatrical, home video while expressly reserving to the writer certain rights that the producer has no interest in or has not bargained for. Publication rights, stage rights, and audio rights are commonly reserved in books, film, and television options, meaning the writer retains the ability to exploit those formats independently even while the option is in effect. The producer's form agreement will not include such reservations and thus they should be negotiated by the rightsholder.

> **PRO TIP:**
>
> All agreements are inherently drafted in favor of the drafter. Thus, it is the recipient's responsibility to even out the provisions, if not tilt in their favor where they have leverage or conviction.

Similarly, shopping agreements as discussed in Chapter 9 involve little or no upfront payment, sometimes include provisions that limit their exclusivity to a specific medium (television only, for instance) or a specific window (no exclusivity for the first sixty days, after which exclusivity attaches if the producer makes a submission). These partial structures can serve a writer's interests when the producer is not willing to pay for full exclusivity, but the writer still wants to allow the relationship to develop. Similarly, a certain medium may not be in the producer's market. It's not uncommon for a writer to have more than one active shopping agreement for a single project, for example, one for scripted and one for unscripted.

A shopping agreement that grants worldwide, all-media exclusivity, for an extended period of time, in exchange for little or no payment should give you pause. Check the producer's track record on past projects. An agreement that takes your exclusivity for free, for an extended period, in exchange only for a promise to 'use best efforts' to set up the project may not be a good deal. If a producer cannot or will not make even a nominal payment for exclusive rights, that is meaningful information about both the producer's resources and the seriousness of their intentions. It's not necessarily a deal killer, but a note to proceed with caution to avoid your project being tied up for some time with one person who may not have the connections they portend to have.

Term

Term is the duration of the agreement for which the producer's rights are in effect, the writer's obligations are in force, and the exclusivity provision runs. It is also the deal point most directly connected to the value of what you are giving up. An option for eighteen months is a different transaction, economically speaking, than an option for five years, even if every other term is identical. The longer the term, the more time your material is off the market, the less flexibility you have to respond to changing circumstances, and the more leverage the producer accumulates simply by virtue of holding the rights.

Term provisions in entertainment agreements typically include three components: the initial period, the extension mechanism, and the outside date or outside drop-dead date after which the agreement expires regardless of what has been accomplished. Understanding all three is essential to evaluating any time-limited agreement.

Initial Period and Extensions

Option agreements typically run for an initial period of twelve to eighteen months to give the producer time to develop a script, assemble a package, and take the project to market. Most agreements include one or more extension options to extend the term for an additional period upon payment of a further option fee. Extensions are usually priced at or above the initial option fee. A producer who has invested in development and generated market interest will almost always exercise an available extension; a producer who has done nothing will sometimes exercise it anyway simply to preserve optionality.

The question for the writer is not just how long the initial period runs, but how long the agreement can run in total if every extension is exercised. An agreement with an eighteen-month initial period, two twelve-month extensions, and a final twelve-month development extension can keep your material locked for four and a half years. Over that period, market conditions change, your own profile may change substantially, and competing projects may close deals on similar material. In addition to the initial period, the total potential duration should be stated clearly in the agreement with each extension to require an affirmative payment rather than a passive right of renewal.

Beware of the rolling extension clause that allows the producer to extend the agreement simply by providing notice, without any additional payment or with a payment so nominal that it functions as an automatic renewal. An extension that costs the producer nothing gives them no incentive to move urgently and gives you no leverage to renegotiate. Extensions should cost something meaningful, and the total potential term of the agreement with all extensions should be a number you are genuinely comfortable with before you sign. If the math adds up to five or six years, that is what you are agreeing to with no recourse if the producer does nothing during that time period.

Suspension Clauses

Many agreements include a suspension clause that pauses the running of the term during defined periods of force majeure, labor strikes, or the writer's own disability or default. Suspension clauses are not inherently abusive and can potentially benefit both parties. There are legitimate reasons for a production to need the clock paused when external circumstances make progress impossible. But a broadly drafted suspension clause can materially extend the effective duration of the agreement beyond what the stated term suggests.

Read any suspension clause carefully and ensure that the grounds for suspension are specific and limited rather than open-ended. An agreement that can be suspended indefinitely for vaguely defined business reasons is an agreement with no meaningful term at all.

Turnaround and Reversion

The end of the term is not always a clean break. Most option and purchase agreements include turnaround provisions that govern what happens when the producer's active development effort cease whether because the option expires, the producer abandons the project, or because specified development milestones are not met within defined periods.

Turnaround and reversion are discussed in more detail in the following chapter, but for now know that the term provision and the reversion mechanism work together. A well-negotiated term provision includes not just a hard expiration date but a defined process for returning rights if the project stalls. This protects the writer from the limbo of a project that is neither actively developed nor formally released.

Price

Price is where the commercial value of the work is most concretely expressed, and it's also where the widest gap lies between what writers expect and what the market can support. Understanding how entertainment deals are priced and what the components of a purchase price means is one of the most practically valuable things a writer can take from this book.

Entertainment rights deals are rarely structured as a single payment. More commonly they involve multiple payment tiers that trigger at different stages of development and production. The option payment, the purchase price, the production bonus, and the sequel and remake payments are distinct components of a deal's overall economic structure. Each one must be negotiated expressly; none of them appears automatically simply because you have agreed to a purchase price.

Option Payments

An option payment is what the producer pays for the right to develop the project during the option period. It is typically a fraction (with ten percent being a standard average) of the agreed purchase price, applied against that purchase price if and when the option is exercised. The phrase *applied against* is important. It means the option payment is not additional compensation; it is an advance on the purchase price, if and when eventually paid. If the purchase price is one hundred thousand dollars and the option payment is ten thousand dollars, exercising the option costs the producer ninety thousand more dollars, not one hundred thousand. You have not received ten thousand dollars on top of the purchase price. You have received it in advance of it.

There is no universally applicable market rate for option payments. In guild-covered deals, the WGA Minimum Basic Agreement (MBA) establishes floors for option payments on covered material (currently 10% of the applicable minimum per 18-month period for theatrical material, and 5% of minimum for the initial 180 days plus 10% per additional 180-day renewal for television material). The floors represent minimums, not necessarily market rates.

On non-guild material, option payments are entirely negotiated. The relevant variables are the nature of the material, the writer's track record, the producer's capitalization and dealmaking history, and whether there is competitive interest from other buyers. A writer who is approached by one producer with no competing offers is in a structurally different negotiating position from a writer whose material is being actively pursued by three production companies simultaneously.

PRO TIP:

For non-WBA writers without a track record, the minimums provided in the WGA Minimum Basic Agreement can be an industry standard guide for pricing a project along with other deal points.

Purchase Price

The purchase price is the total amount payable for the underlying rights upon the producer's exercise of the option. This marks the point at which a development agreement converts into an outright acquisition. Purchase price is almost always expressed as a fixed amount, a percentage of the production budget (typically one to three percent for literary properties), or the greater of those two calculations. Budget-based pricing protects the writer in the event the project scales up significantly between option and production; a flat purchase price locks you into a number that may look very different if the budget doubles. Floors and ceilings can be added in the case of budget-based pricing.

Purchase price is also commonly structured in tranches tied to specific production milestones, for example, a payment upon exercise of the option, an additional payment on commencement of principal photography, and sometimes a final payment on initial release. This structure benefits the producer by spreading payment obligations across the production timeline. It benefits the writer by tying payments to verifiable production events, creating a paper trail of milestones that have been reached. Ensure that the triggering events for each milestone are defined with sufficient precision that you can confirm when they have occurred and enforce payment if the producer delays.

Production Bonuses and Escalators

A production bonus is an additional payment triggered by a specific production achievement that exceeds the baseline development scenario, most commonly upon the commencement of principal photography, or in television, a series order. Production bonuses are negotiated separately from the base purchase price and represent the writer's share of the project's increased commercial value once it becomes an active production rather than a development prospect.

In television, the equivalent mechanism is often an escalator provision that increases the per-episode or per-season payment as the series advances through successive seasons, reflecting the demonstrated commercial viability and the increasing value of the underlying rights of the series. Escalators are standard in television deals; the question is the rate and the cap, both of which are negotiable.

A deal that separates the option payment and the purchase price but omits any provision for a production bonus or escalator is not a red flag, but it should prompt the question of whether the full range of the project's potential value has been contemplated. A purchase price that reflects the value of the material at the time of option may look significantly underpriced if the project ultimately attracts a major director, a significant cast commitment, and a nine-figure production budget. The time to negotiate production bonuses and escalators is before the option is signed, when you still have leverage. Once the option is exercised and the rights are purchased, your ability to renegotiate the economic terms is, for practical purposes, gone.

PRO TIP:

Every agreement by means of a good entertainment attorney should contemplate not only what could go wrong, but also what could go really well for the project in the future.

Separated Rights and Residuals

In guild-covered deals, the WGA MBA provides writers with certain *separated rights* that are retained by the writer even after an outright sale of the underlying material. These include the right to publish a novelization, the right to write a sequel screenplay on a first-priority basis, and various other protections that exist independently of the purchase agreement's express terms. It is worth distinguishing separated rights from reserved rights, two concepts that writers and even some producers commonly conflate. Reserved rights are rights the writer affirmatively carves out of the grant in the option or purchase agreement itself, for example, publication rights, stage rights, audio rights, and other categories the producer is not acquiring. They exist because the contract says so, and if the contract does not say so, they are gone.

Separated rights, by contrast, are creatures of the WGA MBA. They attach automatically to qualifying original material written by a guild writer for a signatory company, regardless of what the individual purchase agreement says. A producer cannot negotiate them away in the deal because they do not arise from the deal. The categories also differ in scope in that reserved rights are whatever the parties agree to reserve, while separated rights are a fixed bundle defined by the MBA and limited to original (not assigned) material.

For a non-guild writer, only reserved rights are available; the separated-rights regime does not apply. For a guild writer working on original material, both layers operate in parallel, and a well-drafted purchase agreement should preserve the separated-rights bundle while also carving out any additional reserved rights the writer wants to retain.

Similarly, residuals are automatically included in the WGA MBA, but not standard in a non-union agreement. *Residuals* are payments to guild writers for the reuse of covered material in supplemental markets, including home video, streaming, and international exhibition. A non-union writer is not without recourse on this point. The economic equivalent to residuals can be replicated contractually, and a writer with any leverage should ask for it. The most common mechanism is a contingent compensation provision that pays the writer a defined percentage of revenues, or a flat per-window fee, when the project is exploited in markets beyond its initial release. A typical formulation might provide the writer a fixed payment upon the project's release in each of several enumerated windows: home video, transactional video on demand, subscription streaming, free television, basic cable, and each major international territory. The figures are negotiated, but the structure mirrors what the MBA imposes on signatory companies.

A second mechanism is a percentage participation in license fees received by the producer from third-party exploitation. If the producer subsequently licenses the project to a streaming platform, a foreign distributor, or a broadcast network, the writer receives a defined percentage of the gross license fee. This is structurally similar to the residuals base under the MBA but is paid directly out of the producer's licensing revenues rather than calculated on guild residual formulas.

When drafting any of these provisions, it's important to include an audit right. Without a guild backstop, the non-union writer's only verification mechanism is the one written into the contract. Writers working on non-guild projects and writers dealing with producers who are not WGA signatories cannot rely on the MBA's protections. The agreement itself must expressly address what the writer retains post-sale. These are provisions worth raising with your entertainment attorney before any purchase agreement is signed.

Backend Participation

No deal point in entertainment is more negotiated, more frequently misunderstood, and more reliably disappointing than backend participation. Backend refers to the writer's contractual right to share in the profits of a project after defined costs and expenses have been recouped from revenues. In concept, it is the writer's equity stake. In other words, it's her participation in the upside if the project succeeds commercially. In practice, it is a provision that delivers real money in some deals and nothing at all in many others.

Backend participation is almost always expressed as a percentage, for example, two percent of net profits, five percent of adjusted gross, one percent of defined gross, and so on. The percentage itself is rarely the most important variable. What matters is the definition of the pool from which that percentage is calculated.

Gross participation is a percentage of gross revenues from the first dollar of receipts and is the gold standard of backend deals available only to A-list talent with sufficient leverage to demand it. Gross participants receive their share from the top of the revenue stack, before any deductions for distribution fees, production costs, overhead, or marketing. Gross participation provisions are highly negotiated, often subject to confidential accounting arrangements, and represent a fundamentally different economic proposition from net profit participation.

Net profit participation is a percentage of profits calculated after an extensive array of deductions and is the standard form of backend participation in most writers' deals. Net profits are calculated by starting with gross revenues and deducting the following: distribution fees (typically twenty to thirty percent of gross, retained by the distributor); distribution expenses (prints, advertising, marketing, and promotion costs, which on major theatrical releases can reach hundreds of millions of dollars); production costs (the negative cost of the film, including all production expenditures); overhead charges (a percentage added by the studio to compensate for its operating infrastructure, typically calculated as fifteen to twenty-five percent of direct production costs); interest on production costs (often charged at a rate above market, accruing from the date each expenditure is incurred); and deferments payable to other participants. What remains, if anything, is net profit.

The practical consequence of this calculation structure is that a film can generate hundreds of millions of dollars in worldwide revenues and still show zero or negative net profits under a studio's standard accounting methodology. In the 1990 *Buchwald v. Paramount* case, the California Superior Court found that the studio's net profit definition was unconscionable as applied to a film that had earned approximately 350 million dollars in worldwide rentals. The practice has been refined but not fundamentally altered in the decades since.

If a producer or studio offers you a net profit participation without defining *net profits* in the agreement, or incorporates by reference a "standard definition," then you have a percentage of a number that may never be positive no matter how successful the project becomes. Understand specifically what is deducted before your percentage is calculated, if for no other reason than to have realistic expectations. The truth is without significant leverage, the net profits definition will not be negotiable, but it should be factored into the total price of the project. A net profit participation in a studio deal can generate net profits, but it is worth materially less than what the percentage suggests, which should be factored into your overall assessment of the deal's economic terms.

PRO TIP:

The Net Profits definition may be defined on an MFN (most favored nations) basis with others within a specific group or 'pool,' meaning you can be assured that your definition will be no less or different than others within that grouping. However, note who the other participants are in the pool, i.e. above-the-line parties, producers, etc., to assure fair treatment.

Between the extremes of true gross and net profit, there are a range of hybrid formulations, i.e. 'adjusted gross,' 'modified adjusted gross,' 'rolling break even,' that are more writer-favorable than net profits but less valuable than true gross. These hybrid pools are calculated before some of the most aggressive net profit deductions (notably overhead and interest) but after others (distribution fees and expenses). The specifics vary from deal to deal and studio to studio. The relevant point for a writer negotiating backend is that the label attached to the participation pool is less informative than the actual definition in the agreement.

In television, backend participation typically takes the form of profit participation in the series rather than the individual episode, with a separate backend pool for streaming and home video exploitation. Television backend accounting has its own definitional complexities — particularly around the studio's retained distribution fees and the treatment of international licensing revenues — that are beyond the scope of this chapter but that your attorney should address when any television deal is on the table.

In independent productions or lower-budget films financed outside the studio system, backend accounting is often less systematically structured but not necessarily more writer-friendly. Independent films frequently have complex waterfall structures governing the order in which multiple investors, lenders, producers, and other participants share in revenues. A writer's backend participation in an independent deal needs to be defined in relation to that waterfall meaning at what point in the revenue distribution does the writer participate, after what recoupment threshold, and in relation to whose calculation of production and distribution costs?

Credit

Credit in the entertainment industry is not merely a matter of professional recognition, it is a contractual right with significant economic consequences that determines residual eligibility, guild benefit entitlements, backend participation thresholds, the writer's market value on the next project, and the durability of her professional reputation over the course of a career. Writers who treat credit as an ego matter rather than a legal and economic issue misunderstand what credit actually does.

How Credit Is Determined

On guild-covered projects, writing credit is determined by the WGA through a formal credit arbitration process governed by its credit determination procedures. The guild makes the final determination of who receives screenplay credit and in what form. Contractual credit provisions in guild deals are therefore subject to WGA determination; a contract that promises sole 'Written by' credit cannot override a guild arbitration that awards that credit differently. Writers should understand that their contractual credit entitlement and their actual credit may diverge on guild-covered projects, and that the WGA's credit determination is the controlling instrument.

On non-guild projects, however, contractual credit provisions are the only operative determination. There is no external governing body, no minimum standards, and no institutional enforcement. The credit goes to whoever the contract says it goes to, subject only to whatever negotiated protections the agreement provides. This makes credit negotiation on non-guild projects both more important and more consequential.

Credit Formulations

"Written by" credit is the most common credit formulation for a produced screenplay, indicating that the credited writer wrote both the story and the screenplay. In guild nomenclature, 'Written by' is awarded when a single writer (or writing team) is responsible for the entire script with no prior material from other sources.

"Screenplay by" credit indicates that the credited writer wrote the screenplay but worked from prior material, such as a novel, article, or prior draft. This differs from 'Story by' credit, which goes to the source material's originator.

"Story by" credit is awarded to a writer who created the underlying story that served as the basis for the screenplay. In adaptation contexts, 'Story by' may be replaced by a source credit such as 'Based on the novel by' or 'Based on an article by.'

"Created by" credit is the television equivalent of "Written by," awarded to the originating writer of a television series and carrying significant economic consequences. The WGA "Created by" credit triggers specific royalty and consultation rights under the MBA that continue for the life of the series.

Credit Placement and Prominence

The visibility and placement of credit is negotiated separately from the credit form. Key contractual specifications include whether credit appears on the main title card or end credits; the relative size of the credit as a percentage of the title of the picture; whether the credit appears in paid advertising (trailers, posters, print campaigns); and whether the credit is on a separate card or shared with other names. Sole card credit with only one name, on its own screen, is more valuable than shared card credit. Main title placement is more valuable than end credits. Paid advertising inclusion is more valuable than screen-only credit.

Studios negotiate credit placement provisions carefully and in their own favor. Form agreements typically give the producer maximum discretion over advertising credit placement, often including a broad carve-out for "award consideration" advertising, "teaser" advertising, and other formats in which writer credit is routinely omitted. The carve-outs are largely standard, but the overall inclusion of advertising credit is worth negotiating explicitly.

An agreement that does not specify the form, placement, and size of credit and simply states you are entitled to "credit in accordance with industry custom" or "credit as determined by producer" provides essentially no enforceable credit protection. Credit provisions should be specific and include the form of the credit (i.e. Written by, Created by), where it appears (i.e. main title, end credits), whether it appears in paid advertising, in what size relative to the title, and on what card (i.e. single or shared).

Economic Consequences of Credit

The economic stakes of credit extend well beyond professional recognition. WGA residual payments are calculated based on credited writers; a writer who receives credit is eligible for residuals from the picture's exploitation in supplemental markets, while a writer who does not receive credit is not. Production bonuses and escalators are frequently tied to credit, for example, a higher bonus triggers if the writer receives sole screenplay credit than if credit is shared. Backend participation thresholds and priority positions in the revenue waterfall sometimes track credit as well.

In television, "Created by" credit carries the most significant long-term economic consequences. The credited creator receives royalties for every episode produced, consultation rights on casting and scripts, and, in many cases, a contractually guaranteed role as executive producer for the duration of the series. On a successful series, "Created by" royalties alone can generate substantial ongoing income. Protecting that credit in a clean, express, enforceable contractual provision, and through the WGA's credit determination process if the project is guild-covered is among the most economically consequential things a television writer can do.

Guild Production with Non-Guild Writer

A common scenario is when a WGA signatory wants to develop and produce a non-union writer's screenplay. The production itself would in effect qualify the writer to become a WGA member. The WGA MBA requires that any signatory company use only guild writers on covered projects, with a narrow exception that allows a signatory to engage a non-member writer for up to thirty days, after which the writer must join the guild to continue working. In effect, the first guild-covered job a non-union writer takes is, by operation of the MBA, the job that makes her a member.

The contractual consequences are significant and frequently misunderstood by writers entering this situation for the first time. Once the project is set up at a signatory company, the MBA applies to the writer's deal whether the writer is a guild member at the moment of signing or not. That means the writer is entitled to the MBA minimums for whatever services and rights the signatory is acquiring, the option-payment floors discussed earlier in this chapter, the separated-rights bundle on original material, residuals, pension and health contributions, and the credit-arbitration protections that accompany guild status. A signatory company cannot offer a non-member writer a deal at sub-MBA terms simply because the writer is not yet in the guild. The signatory's own status as a guild company carries the MBA floors with it. This creates a leverage moment that the writer should recognize.

If a non-signatory producer has the writer's screenplay under option or shopping arrangement and subsequently sets up the project at a signatory studio, the writer's deal terms are likely to be revised upward to comply with MBA minimums as a condition of the signatory's involvement. The writer who signed a non-union deal at terms below MBA floors is not bound to those terms once the project enters the guild ecosystem; the signatory company's execution of the writer's deal must conform to the MBA, and the writer's pre-existing agreement is, in practical effect, superseded to the extent of any conflict with guild minimums. A non-union writer in this position should not assume the original terms travel with the project. They typically do not, and the moment the signatory takes over is the moment to negotiate the upgrade explicitly rather than rely on the signatory to volunteer it.

Three practical points warrant attention when a non-union writer is approached by a signatory or a producer who intends to set the project up at one. First, do not sign a non-union deal in anticipation of a signatory acquisition without preserving the right to renegotiate when the project becomes guild-covered. A clause stating that the writer's compensation, credit, and rights provisions will be conformed to MBA minimums upon any guild-covered production is straightforward to negotiate at the front end and difficult to negotiate after the fact. Second, understand that joining the guild is not optional once the writer accepts a signatory job that exceeds the thirty-day window. Initiation fees and dues become payable, and the writer's subsequent work must conform to guild rules including the prohibition on writing for non-signatory companies.

Third, recognize that guild membership is, on balance, a significant career asset for a working writer. The MBA's separated-rights, residuals structure, credit-arbitration process, and pension and health contributions are economically material, and the access they provide to the established professional infrastructure of the industry is difficult to replicate through individual contract negotiation. The non-union writer who is offered a path into the guild through a signatory production is generally being offered something worth more than the membership obligations it imposes.

How the Deal Points Interact

These five provisions discussed—exclusivity, term, price, backend, and credit—do not operate in isolation. They are interdependent variables in a negotiation where improvement in one dimension often requires compromise in another. Understanding the trade-off structure is as important as understanding each provision individually.

Exclusivity and term interact directly with broader exclusivity and longer terms command higher prices because the writer is giving up more. A producer who asks for worldwide, all-media exclusivity for five years is asking for something materially more valuable than a producer asking for North American television exclusivity for eighteen months. The pricing should reflect that difference, and if it does not, the terms should be narrowed.

Price and backend interact in the opposite direction. In many negotiations, a higher upfront purchase price and strong backend participation are inversely related. A producer with limited capital may offer more favorable backend terms in exchange for a reduced upfront payment, betting that the project's commercial success will make the backend valuable. A well-capitalized buyer may prefer a higher upfront payment and weaker backend terms. Which structure serves the writer better depends on the specific project, the producer's track record, and the writer's own assessment of the project's commercial potential. There is no universally correct answer. Instead, the question is what is the expected value of this deal across the realistic range of outcomes?

Credit and price intersect in deals where the purchase price or production bonus escalates based on credit received. A deal that pays significantly more for sole credit than for shared credit creates a significant incentive. It means the producer has agreed, in advance, that sole credit is worth more, but has structured the economic benefit to flow to a future event that may be determined by factors outside your control.

Deal Point	What It Controls	Key Variables to Negotiate	Common Red Flag	Writer's Core Goal
Exclusivity	What you can do with the material (or your time) during the agreement	Territory, media, whether partial exclusivity is available	Worldwide all-media exclusivity for no payment	Narrow scope; ensure payment proportionate to restriction

Deal Point	What It Controls	Key Variables to Negotiate	Common Red Flag	Writer's Core Goal
Term	How long the agreement runs; how long your rights are off the market	Initial period, number and cost of extensions, total potential duration, suspension clauses	Rolling extensions that cost nothing; broadly drafted suspension provisions	Hard cap on total duration; paid extensions; defined reversion on inactivity
Price	Upfront option payments, purchase price, production bonuses	Budget-based vs. fixed pricing, milestone tranches, production bonus triggers	Fixed flat price with no escalator and no production bonus	Budget-tied price, defined milestones, production bonus on photography
Backend	Participation in profits after production and distribution	Definition of the profit pool; position in the waterfall; gross vs. net vs. adjusted gross	Net profit participation with undefined or undefined-by-reference profit definition	Read and negotiate the definition; prefer adjusted gross or gross where possible
Credit	Form, placement, size, and advertising inclusion of your professional credit	Credit form, card position, paid advertising inclusion, size relative to title	Credit 'as determined by producer' or 'in accordance with industry custom'	Specific, express credit provision; WGA credit protection on guild projects

Keep in mind that not every problematic provision is a deal killer. A first-time writer dealing with a well-capitalized studio is not in the same negotiating position as an established showrunner. But leverage is also more widely distributed than writers typically assume. The producer who wants your material badly enough to option it is the producer who needs something from you.

Understand that these five deal points are not a substitute for competent legal representation. An entertainment attorney who regularly handles these transactions will recognize provisions that do not appear in this chapter, will understand the specific customs and practices of studios and financiers, and will bring negotiating relationships and institutional knowledge that no book can replicate. What this chapter gives you is the vocabulary and the framework to participate meaningfully in that representation and to know what to ask about, to identify what is missing, and to understand what you are agreeing to when you sign.

The chapter that follows addresses two deal points that warrant extended treatment beyond this chapter's framework: reversion, and the trio of sequels, remakes, and derivative works. These provisions determine not just what happens during the deal, but what happens to your material after it.

CHAPTER 13

LONG-TERM DEAL POINTS

Imagine this scenario: A writer sells the option on her screenplay to an enthusiastic producer; the deal terms feel fair, and the option purchase price, while modest, reflects the realities of an early-stage project. The agreement is signed and then… nothing. Months pass. The producer's emails become infrequent, then sparse, then nonexistent. Two years later, the writer learns, from a mutual acquaintance, that the producer has shifted focus to an entirely different genre. The screenplay sits in a filing cabinet, unproduced and unavailable. She cannot sell it to anyone else. She cannot develop it herself. She cannot even publish it as a novel. The option has not been exercised, but the agreement contains no reversion provision, and the option period, as extended by the producer's timely exercise of extension payments, still has eighteen months to run.

Variations of this story play out regularly in the entertainment industry because the provisions that would have prevented it are among the most frequently under negotiated, or simply omitted, deal points in agreements between writers and producers. They are addressed late in negotiations, when deal fatigue has set in and both parties are eager to close. They are dismissed as speculative and they are obscured by language that sounds reassuring in the abstract but is effectively unenforceable in practice. This chapter provides an understanding of those rights and how to negotiate them with the precision and foresight they require.

Reversion

A reversion provision is a contractual mechanism by which rights that have been conveyed to a producer, studio, or other acquiring party return, or revert back, to the original owner upon the occurrence of specified conditions. In most contexts, those conditions relate to the failure of the acquiring party to exercise the rights it has obtained within a defined period or in accordance with defined milestones. Reversion is the writer's insurance policy against a project dying quietly in development while the rights to exploit it remain locked up indefinitely.

The analogy to real property is again instructive. In certain real estate transactions, a grantor may convey property subject to a condition subsequent—a clause providing that title automatically returns to the grantor if the grantee fails to use the property for a specified purpose. Reversion provisions in entertainment agreements operate on a similar conceptual basis. The conveyance is real, but it is not unconditional, and if the conditions subsequent are not satisfied, the rights return home.

It is important to distinguish reversion from the automatic termination rights that exist under copyright law. Section 203 of Title 17 of the United States Code provides authors and their statutory heirs with a right to terminate grants of copyright (made on or after January 1, 1978) within a statutory window beginning thirty-five years after the date of the grant. This termination right is non-waivable; it cannot be contracted away, and it applies regardless of what the agreement says. That right, however, is a creature of statute with its own procedural requirements, its own timing constraints, and its own limitations. It is not a substitute for a carefully negotiated contractual reversion provision, which operates on *a much shorter timeline* and does not require the writer to wait decades before asserting it.

When a Writer Encounters Reversion

Reversion provisions appear or should appear in every agreement in which a writer transfers or licenses rights to a third party in connection with the development or production of a film or television project. That means shopping agreements, option agreements, option-purchase agreements, and literary purchase agreements. In each of these instruments, the writer has conveyed, at minimum, the exclusive right to develop and sell the project during the option period and, at maximum, a full assignment of copyright. In each case, the writer has an interest in ensuring that the transfer does not become permanent by default simply because the producer fails to act.

In a shopping agreement, the producer has obtained a limited right to pitch the project. A reversion provision here typically operates as a sunset so that if the producer has not placed the project with a buyer within the shopping period, the right to shop terminates and the writer is free to take it elsewhere. In an option agreement, reversion becomes more critical. The writer has granted an exclusive right that may effectively freeze the project for months or years. If the option is not exercised, the rights revert at the end of the option period; but if the agreement contains extension provisions allowing the producer to extend the option term by payment, the reversion may be deferred far longer than the writer anticipated.

In a purchase agreement, the producer has acquired the underlying rights outright, and reversion is typically conditioned on far more specific production milestones. The version of reversion that writers most urgently need, and most commonly fail to secure, is production-based reversion. This is the right to reclaim the purchased rights if the producer fails to commence principal photography within a defined period after the purchase. This is sometimes also referred to as a turnaround right.

Reversion Triggers

Reversion provisions are defined almost entirely by their trigger conditions, that is, the specific events that, if they do not occur within a defined period, cause the rights to revert. There are two primary categories of trigger: development triggers and production triggers. Each addresses different risks and operates on different timelines.

Development triggers condition reversion on the producer's failure to engage in meaningful development activity within a defined period after the execution of the agreement or after the expiration of the initial option term. "Development activity" and "active development" are vague terms that should be more specifically defined in order to have any real effect. A producer can always point to some nominal activity, for example, a meeting, an email exchange, a submission to a talent agency, as evidence of active development. A well-drafted development trigger specifies concrete, measurable milestones, such as the attachment of a director or showrunner of a defined credit level, commencement of a writers' room, delivery of a revised draft, receipt of a network commitment, or similar. The more specific the milestone and the shorter the timeline for achieving it, the more protective the provision.

Production triggers condition reversion on the producer's failure to commence principal photography within a specified period. This is the reversion provision that most directly addresses the risk of a project being purchased and then buried. The critical drafting question is what constitutes "commencement of principal photography." Producers will often argue that a first-day-of-photography standard is appropriate; writers should push for a rolling commencement requirement that cannot be satisfied by a single day's shooting followed by an indefinite hiatus. The WGA's standard turnaround provisions, which apply to covered agreements, provide useful benchmarks for non-guild writers negotiating analogous provisions.

PRO TIP:

A reversion provision that defines its trigger by reference to the producer's "good faith efforts" to develop or produce the project is a red flag. Insist on objective, measurable triggers with fixed deadlines.

The Price of a Turnaround

When a reversion occurs in the context of a purchase agreement where the producer has paid the writer for the underlying rights the reversion is typically not free. The writer may be obligated to reimburse the producer for some, or all, of the consideration paid for the rights, plus, in some negotiations, a portion of the development costs the producer has incurred. This buyback mechanism is what the industry calls the *turnaround price*.

`The turnaround price is one of the most consequential and frequently misunderstood elements of a reversion provision. A writer who negotiates a reversion trigger without also negotiating a reasonable turnaround price may find that the right to reclaim her work is technically available but practically inaccessible particularly if the turnaround price includes not just the original purchase price but also accumulated development expenditures, overhead allocations, and interest. Whether the option payment itself is included in the turnaround price is a negotiated point. Because the option payment is typically applied against the purchase price upon exercise, a producer who has exercised will usually seek to recover it as part of turnaround, while a writer should push to exclude any unexercised option payments and, where possible, to cap recoverable amounts at documented, out-of-pocket development costs. An unreasonable turnaround price effectively converts the reversion right into a right of first refusal by a different name. In other words, the producer knows the writer cannot pay, and so the rights are practically irretrievable.

Effective negotiation of turnaround terms should address at minimum the following variables: the base turnaround price (typically the amount paid by the producer for the rights, plus or minus a negotiated premium or discount); whether and to what extent development costs are included in the turnaround calculation; whether the turnaround price is fixed or escalates over time; and whether the writer has the right to assign the turnaround obligation to a third party, for example, a new producer who wishes to take over the project, rather than paying it out of pocket. This last point is particularly important because the most common mechanism by which writers exercise turnaround rights is by finding a new buyer for the project who assumes the turnaround obligation as part of a new deal.

In some cases, rather than requiring the writer or a successor producer to repay the turnaround amount upfront, the original producer will accept a lien against the future project, allowing the turnaround obligation to be satisfied out of the project's first proceeds if and when it is set up elsewhere and produced. This structure can make a project meaningfully easier to set up at a new home, because the successor producer is not required to come out of pocket at the moment of acquisition. This sets up a win-win scenario for the writer, previous producer, and new production.

Cure Periods and Waiver Risks

Most reversion provisions include a cure period in the form of a defined window during which the producer may remedy a reversion trigger after notice from the writer. Cure periods allow a producer who is in technical default but actively working toward the triggering milestone to avoid losing the project on a technicality. But they also create risk for writers who fail to provide timely notice or who waive their reversion rights through conduct.

A writer who is aware that a reversion trigger has occurred but continues to accept development payments, participate in production meetings, or otherwise behave as though the project is proceeding normally may be deemed to have waived the right to assert reversion. Courts have found implied waivers in circumstances where the party asserting the right engaged in conduct inconsistent with its intent to enforce. The practical lesson is that reversion rights, like options, require affirmative and timely exercise. If you believe a trigger has occurred, you must assert it in writing, preferably through counsel, within whatever notice period the agreement provides.

Sequels, Remakes, and Spin-Offs

When a producer acquires rights to a screenplay or underlying literary work, the acquisition agreement will typically include a grant of rights that extends well beyond the original production. That grant will almost invariably encompass the rights to create sequels, prequels, remakes, and spin-offs based on the acquired material. These rights are sometimes referred to collectively as allied and ancillary rights, and they can be a potentially enormous source of value in a commercially successful project.

Writers often treat these provisions as aspirational boilerplate. Why worry about sequel rights before the first film is even greenlit? But the time to negotiate sequel, remake, and spin-off provisions is in the original agreement, or else they will be thrown in for free with the price of the original project. Let's look at each of these rights in more detail.

Sequel Rights

A sequel right is the producer's contractual ability to create a subsequent narrative work in the format of a film, television series, or other production that continues, extends, or builds upon the story, characters, or world established in the original. In a standard industry agreement, the grant of sequel rights is often framed in broad, catch-all terms: "all sequel rights in perpetuity throughout the universe in any and all media now known or hereafter devised." That language, once accepted, is extraordinarily difficult to constrain after the fact.

The writer's primary interest in negotiating sequel rights is not, typically, to withhold them. A producer will rarely acquire a project without sequel rights, and insisting on their retention is unlikely to be productive in most negotiations. The writer's interest is, rather, to ensure that she is fairly compensated for each sequel produced, receives credit commensurate with her contribution to the franchise, and is afforded meaningful participation in the creative process of any subsequent works that draw on her original material.

Compensation for sequel rights typically takes one of two forms: a fixed sequel fee, payable each time a sequel is produced, stated as a percentage of the original purchase price or as a negotiated flat amount; or a step-up, in which the sequel fee increases by a defined percentage with each successive sequel. Writers should negotiate for both a reasonable minimum and an escalation mechanism. For example, a franchise that generates three sequels has proven its commercial value, and the original writer's participation should reflect that.

The separated rights framework established by the WGA's Minimum Basic Agreement provides a useful baseline for understanding what protections exist in a guild context. Under separated rights, a writer who has performed a specified minimum of work on a script may retain certain separated rights, including novelization rights, theatrical rights, and limited sequel rights, even after the screenplay has been purchased by a studio. Non-WGA writers do not receive these protections automatically and must negotiate for comparable provisions contractually. The existence of the guild framework underscores that these are real and negotiable interests, not aspirational ones.

PRO TIP:

An agreement that grants the producer sequel rights without specifying the writer's compensation for each sequel entitles the writer to nothing when those sequels are produced. Negotiate the future economics before you sign the original deal.

Remake Rights

A remake right entitles the producer to re-produce the same underlying story with the same narrative, with the same general structure and characters in a new production. Remakes are distinguished from sequels in that they do not continue or extend the original narrative; they restart it, typically with a new cast, new director, and often updated setting or tone. The legal and commercial distinction matters because the compensation structures and credit implications are different.

From a writer's perspective, a remake is in some respects more threatening than a sequel. A sequel extends her franchise; a remake may effectively replace her original work with a new version over which she has no creative input and from which she may derive no economic benefit, depending on how her agreement is drafted. A producer who acquires remake rights without negotiating the writer's participation in remake productions has acquired the ability to build an entirely new creative enterprise on the foundation of the writer's original contribution, without any obligation to the writer beyond whatever the original acquisition agreement requires.

The appropriate negotiating position is to treat remake rights as a separate bundle with its own compensation terms. A remake fee is typically expressed as a percentage of the original purchase price, often in the range of thirty-three to fifty percent and should be specified, along with a credit obligation that acknowledges the original writer's contribution to the source material. Writers should also explore whether the agreement can include a first-negotiation right for writing the remake screenplay before engaging another screenwriter for the remake.

Spin-Off Rights

A spin-off is a production derived not from the original story as a whole, but from specific elements of it, most commonly, from characters developed in the original work. A spin-off takes a character from the original film or series and builds a new narrative around that character, typically in a separate production with its own story arc. The distinction between a spin-off and a sequel is meaningful in that a spin-off does not continue the original story; it branches from it, using a specific creative element as its foundation.

The significance of this distinction for writers is considerable. If a writer creates an original and distinctive character whose personality, backstory, voice, and dramatic function are primarily the product of the writer's creative work, then a spin-off production built around that character is, in a meaningful artistic sense, a new work that derives its core creative value from the writer's contribution. The extent to which the writer is compensated for that contribution depends entirely on the spin-off provisions in her agreement.

Character ownership is the central question in spin-off negotiations, and it is among the most contested. Producers will argue that the character as it appears in a produced film is not purely the writer's creation; it has been shaped by casting, performance, direction, and dozens of other creative inputs. Writers will argue that the character's defining traits, voice, and dramatic function were fixed in the screenplay before any of those inputs were applied. Both positions have merit, and the resolution, in litigation, depends heavily on the facts of the specific case.

Writers of original characters should push for explicit spin-off participation provisions, including a fee per spin-off project, a credit obligation, and, where feasible, a consultation right with respect to the character's depiction in the new work. The most valuable characters in entertainment history are the ones that have generated the most enduring franchise value and were almost always created by writers. The spin-off provisions in the original acquisition agreements governing those characters ultimately determine whether the writer who created them participated in that value at all.

In a related matter, characters can be protected as a matter of intellectual property law. Copyright protects a character that is sufficiently distinctive and well-developed in its expression, meaning a character whose personality, appearance, and dramatic function are delineated with enough specificity to constitute original authorship rather than a stock type. The character in a book or script would be included in the underlying copyright filing, or in a separate copyright filing, if desired.

Trademark, by contrast, protects the commercial identity of a character whose name and distinctive visual elements have come to identify a particular source in the marketplace, such as a franchise character whose silhouette, costume, or catchphrase functions as a brand signifier. The copyright in the work eventually expires, while trademark rights, if continuously used in commerce and properly maintained, can endure indefinitely. A character may therefore carry copyright protection, trademark protection, both, or neither, and the strength of the writer's negotiating position on spin-off rights is meaningfully shaped by which of those protections actually attach to the character at issue.

PRO TIP:

Trademarking a character created or partially created using AI can be used to protect a mark that would otherwise not by copyrightable due to the use of AI.

Derivative Works

Copyright law defines a derivative work as a work based upon one or more preexisting works, including a translation, musical arrangement, dramatization, fictionalization, motion picture version, sound recording, art reproduction, abridgment, condensation, or any other form in which a work may be recast, transformed, or adapted. This definition, codified at 17 U.S.C. § 101, is deliberately broad. The right to create derivative works is one of the exclusive rights comprising the copyright bundle under 17 U.S.C. § 106, and it can be conveyed in whole or in part by assignment or license.

In the context of an entertainment agreement, a grant of derivative works rights is, in practical effect, a grant of the broadest possible exploitation authority. A producer who holds the derivative works right to a screenplay can create not just the original film, but a stage adaptation, a novelization, a graphic novel, a video game, a theme park attraction, and any other form in which the underlying story can be recast or transformed. The derivative works right subsumes, in effect, sequels, remakes, and spin-offs as they are, technically, derivative works. When producers request a grant that includes derivative works rights without specifying the scope of that grant, they are often seeking a catch-all that will capture anything not covered by the enumerated rights.

The breadth of the derivative works right creates an overreach problem that writers and their attorneys must address with precision. A grant of "all derivative works rights" in a screenplay acquisition agreement may operate to transfer to the producer not only the right to produce the film, but the right to exploit the writer's underlying creative work—her characters, her narrative structure, her thematic framework—in every conceivable medium, in perpetuity, throughout the universe.

As discussed in earlier chapters, the label given to a particular agreement is irrelevant. What matters is the operative language of the agreement, the specific definition of the rights transferred and the specific exclusions, carve-outs, and the limitations that are negotiated into the document. A writer who reviews a purchase agreement and sees "all derivative works rights" in the grant clause must ask: derivative works of what? In what media? For what territory? For what term? With what compensation? And with what carve-outs retained?

The retained rights that writers most commonly seek to carve out from a derivative works grant include novelization rights, which allow the writer to publish a novel based on her original screenplay; stage rights, which allow her to develop a theatrical adaptation; and, in some cases, limited interactive or gaming rights. These carve-outs are not always available, particularly in large studio deals where the acquiring party's leverage is substantial, but they represent legitimate creative and economic interests that a writer should at least attempt to protect.

Derivative Works in Television

The derivative works landscape is particularly complex in television, where a single original series may generate not only subsequent seasons, which are typically treated as extensions of the original license rather than separate derivative works, but also international format rights, foreign-language adaptations, and platform-specific versions. Writers creating original television series should attend carefully to the distinction between rights in the original series format and rights in specific episodes or story elements that they have personally contributed. The WGA's separated rights framework provides specific protections in this regard, including a reserved right to receive payment for any television spin-off based on a character the writer created, but again, these protections apply only in covered situations.

Non-guild writers and writers whose agreements are structured as direct acquisition deals rather than employment agreements must negotiate equivalent protections expressly. An original series creator who conveys derivative works rights without carving out format rights, international adaptation rights, or platform-specific version rights may find that the producer is able to license the show's format to a foreign broadcaster, or to a competing streaming platform, without any obligation to the original creator.

Reserved Rights

The practical approach to derivative works provisions is to start from the position that the grant should be limited to the rights actually necessary for the contemplated production, and to require that any additional derivative works rights be separately negotiated. This is rarely achievable in a major studio deal, where the acquiring party will insist on a comprehensive rights package. In such a case, the price should be adjusted accordingly. It is more commonly achievable in independent film and lower-budget television contexts, where the leverage differential is less extreme and the producer's legitimate need for ancillary rights is more modest.

In either case, a reserved rights clause is helpful to expressly carve out from the grant any rights not specifically conveyed to the producer. Without such a clause, an ambiguously drafted grant that includes broad catch-all language such as "all rights in and to the Work" or "all derivative works rights" may be construed to sweep in rights the writer never intended to transfer, including publication rights, stage rights, audio and podcast rights, merchandising rights, live performance rights, interactive and gaming rights, and rights in media not yet invented. The reserved rights clause closes that interpretive gap by stating affirmatively, in the writer's own voice within the agreement, that all rights not expressly granted are reserved. Insisting on an express reserved rights provision is one of the most cost-effective protections a writer can negotiate, and it is one that producers will generally accept once the principle is raised.

Provision	**What It Grants / Protects**	**Key Negotiating Lever**	**Writer's Priority**
Reversion	Right to reclaim rights if producer fails to develop or produce	Trigger events; cure period length; purchase price on reclaim	High — prevents permanent burial of project
Reversion — Development Trigger	Reclaim if project not in active development within set period	Definition of "active development"; milestone specificity	High

Provision	What It Grants / Protects	Key Negotiating Lever	Writer's Priority
Reversion — Production Trigger	Reclaim if production not commenced within set period	Definition of "principal photography"; turnaround price	High
Sequel Rights	Producer's right to create follow-on narrative works	Writer's participation fee and credit per sequel	Medium — negotiate payment floors
Remake Rights	Right to re-produce the same story in a new production	Fee as percentage of original; separated rights on remake screenplay	Medium — often overlooked
Spin-Off Rights	Right to develop ancillary works based on characters or elements	Character ownership; participation fee per spin-off project	High if original characters are distinctive
Derivative Works	Broad right to create adaptations, translations, dramatizations	Scope of definition; carve-outs for retained rights	Critical — broadest grant; most susceptible to overreach

The deal points addressed in this chapter are contemplated years or decades in advance. A writer who signs an agreement in year one may not encounter the practical consequences of her reversion provision until year three, or her sequel fee until year five, or the scope of her derivative works grant until the project has generated enough franchise value that the stakes are impossible to ignore. By that time, the agreement has long since been finalized and the leverage has long since shifted, and the language controls. As such, it's easy to dismiss them as speculative when you are sitting across the table from a producer who is enthusiastic about your project and eager to close. It is much harder to dismiss them when you are watching the franchise built on your original work generate tens of millions of dollars in ancillary revenue, none of which you are receiving.

The principles in this chapter are standard professional practice for writers who understand that their creative work is an asset with long-term commercial potential, and that the agreements they sign today will govern the exploitation of that asset for as long as copyright law protects it. Therefore, approaching these provisions from the dealmaker's posture means recognizing that the producer across the table has every incentive to acquire as many rights as possible, for as long as possible, at as low a price as possible. Your protection against that outcome is the specific, negotiated language of a carefully drafted agreement. The boilerplate provisions discussed in the next chapter are tempting to gloss over, however, they too are no different in determining the future outcome of your work.

ACT VI

The Fine Print

Marcus had spent three years developing an independent feature, optioning underlying rights, attaching a director, assembling financing from four separate sources. The production agreement had been negotiated carefully. The major deal points had been the subject of extended back-and-forth: purchase price, producing credit, backend participation, the reversion mechanics if the film was not delivered within a specified period. All of it had been reviewed, revised, and ultimately agreed to. What no one had spent much time on was Section 19.

Section 19 was the boilerplate — force majeure, warranties and indemnification, choice of law, dispute resolution. These are the provisions that every experienced entertainment attorney knows are consequential and that every exhausted party, at the end of a long negotiation, is tempted to treat as standard. They had been negotiated quickly, without significant pushback, on the theory that they were unlikely to matter.

When a global supply chain disruption halted production mid-shoot and the primary financier attempted to invoke force majeure to suspend its payment obligations indefinitely, Section 19 became the most important section in the agreement. The force majeure definition was broad. The carve-outs Marcus's attorney had proposed and been asked to drop—provisions that would have limited the suspension period and required demonstrated causation—were not there. The dispute resolution clause required arbitration in a jurisdiction that favored the financier. The indemnification provision was mutual on its face but structured in a way that allocated substantially more exposure to Marcus.

The production resumed and the dispute eventually resolved. But the resolution cost Marcus fourteen months, a directing attachment that walked, and a legal bill that absorbed a meaningful portion of his backend.

CHAPTER 14

THE BOILERPLATE TERMS

The purchase price is set, the option period is defined, the sequel fees are specified, the credit obligations are agreed upon, and all key deal points have been papered with both sides ready to close. What remains are a dozen or so provisions near the back of the agreement, dense with legal language and abstract conditions, commonly referred to as the *boilerplate*. It is the section of the contract that gets skimmed over on the theory that it is standard, that it is the same in every agreement, and that it does not really affect the deal. However, those assumptions are wrong.

The boilerplate provisions addressed in this chapter address what happens when things go wrong; for example, when a third party claims the writer infringed their copyright, when a global pandemic shuts down production, when the producer and the writer disagree about whether a reversion has been triggered, or when a dispute escalates to the point of formal legal proceedings. In each of those scenarios, the outcome is governed not by the deal points the parties negotiated with care, but by the provisions they quickly scrolled through. This chapter is about understanding those provisions in order to have the vocabulary and foresight to understand what's at stake in any individual negotiation.

Warranties and Indemnification

What Warranties Are

In contracts, a warranty is a representation of fact made by one party to another as an inducement to enter the agreement. In entertainment agreements, the warranties that writers are asked to make are typically clustered into a single, densely worded paragraph near the end of the document but extend to every other provision of the contract. When a writer signs an agreement containing a warranty, she is not merely making a promise; she is making a statement of existing fact that, if false, constitutes a breach of contract regardless of her intent or knowledge at the time of signing.

In a standard warranties provision in a literary acquisition or option agreement, the writer will be asked to represent that she is the sole author of the work; that the work is original and does not infringe the copyright, trademark, right of publicity, or any other intellectual property right of any third party; that the work does not defame any person or entity; that she has the full right, power, and authority to enter the agreement and to grant the rights conveyed therein; that the work has not previously been optioned, sold, or otherwise encumbered in any manner inconsistent with the agreement; and that no litigation, claim, or threatened claim exists with respect to the work. Each of these representations is a warranty and carries with it an indemnification obligation if it proves to be false.

The Warranty of Originality

The warranty of originality is the one that creates the most practical risk for writers, and it is the one that demands the most careful attention. When a writer represents that her screenplay is original and does not infringe any third-party rights, she is making an absolute representation that she wrote the script. A writer who unconsciously reproduces protected expression from a work she read years earlier, without any awareness that she has done so, has breached her originality warranty if that reproduction constitutes copyright infringement. Good faith is not a defense to warranty breach; it may be relevant to damages, but it does not eliminate the breach itself.

This is not a reason to refuse to make an originality warranty as such a refusal would certainly kill the deal. It is a reason to understand precisely what the warranty covers and to negotiate appropriate qualifications. The most important qualification is a knowledge limitation. Rather than warranting that the work does not infringe any third-party rights in an absolute sense, the writer should warrant only that, "to the best of her actual knowledge," the work does not infringe. This parenthetical differentiates between absolute liability for any infringement, regardless of culpability, and liability limited to situations in which the writer actually knew of a problem and proceeded anyway.

A second critical qualification applies when the screenplay is based on underlying source material that has been separately licensed. If the writer has adapted a novel, a published article, a podcast, or any other protected work pursuant to a properly negotiated underlying rights agreement, her warranty of originality should expressly carve out that underlying material. She is warranting the originality of her contribution, not the originality of the underlying work, which is the responsibility of the party who cleared the underlying rights. Failing to negotiate this carve-out may result in the writer warranting the originality of source material that was never hers to vouch for.

A third qualification that is rapidly evolving is the writer's use of generative AI in the creation of the screenplay. Because the United States Copyright Office requires human authorship as a condition of copyright registration, material generated by AI without sufficient human creative contribution is not protectable by copyright. This has direct consequences for chain of title. A screenplay containing meaningful AI-generated material may be only partially copyrightable, and thus the producer who acquires the work may find that portions of what she paid for cannot be registered, cannot be defended against third-party copying, and cannot be insured under an errors-and-omissions policy without a specific AI rider. In response, producers are increasingly adding AI-specific representations to the warranties provision.

The most common formulations require the writer to represent that no part of the work was generated by AI, or alternatively to disclose any AI use and warrant that all AI-generated portions have been sufficiently revised, edited, or transformed by the writer to constitute original human authorship. Sophisticated agreements will go further and require a warranty that any AI tools used by the writer were not trained on infringing material, shifting that diligence obligation back onto the writer or the AI vendor. The WGA's 2023 Minimum Basic Agreement layers a separate disclosure obligation onto guild-covered writers, but the contractual warranty operates independently and applies regardless of guild status. Writers should approach the use of AI in their work in a similar fashion as the use of any third-party materials for purposes of the originality warranty provision. More importantly, the warranties provision shouldn't be glossed over as boilerplate as it constitutes an important element in chain of title.

What Indemnification Is

Indemnification is the mechanism by which the consequences of a warranty breach, or of a third-party claim arising from the subject matter of the agreement, are allocated between the parties. An indemnification clause requires one party (the indemnitor) to compensate the other (the indemnitee) for losses, costs, expenses, and attorneys' fees incurred as a result of a defined category of claims. In entertainment agreements, the writer is almost invariably the indemnitor with respect to claims arising from the content of her work, and the producer is the indemnitee. That allocation is not inherently unreasonable because the writer is in the best position to know whether her work is original. However, the scope and mechanics of the indemnification obligation require careful negotiation and should not be completely one-sided in favor of the producer.

The threshold question in any indemnification negotiation is what triggers the obligation? The broadest and most producer-favorable formulation triggers indemnification upon the mere assertion of a claim, that is, the moment a third party files a complaint or sends a demand letter alleging that the writer's work infringes their rights. At that point, the indemnification mechanism activates, and the writer would be required to fund the producer's defense costs, regardless of whether the claim has any merit. This is an extraordinary obligation, and it is one that writers should resist. A meritless claim, pursued by a litigant with nothing to lose, can generate hundreds of thousands of dollars in defense costs that the writer would be required to advance while the claim is pending, before any determination of its validity has been made.

The better alternative is to condition indemnification on a final, non-appealable adverse judgment or settlement to which the writer has consented. Under this formulation, the writer's indemnification obligation does not arise until a competent tribunal has determined that the claim was valid, or until the writer has agreed that the claim should be resolved by settlement. The writer is not required to fund the defense of claims that may ultimately be dismissed, and she retains meaningful control over whether a settlement is entered on her behalf. This formulation is sometimes resisted by producers who argue that it leaves them exposed during the pendency of a long-running dispute. The response is that it leaves them in the same position they would be in without an indemnification clause which is the appropriate baseline.

Defense Costs and the Right to Control Litigation

Two subsidiary issues in indemnification negotiation deserve specific attention: who controls the defense of a third-party claim, and who funds it during the pendency of the proceeding. Control of the defense matters because the party controlling the defense controls the litigation strategy and the litigation strategy determines, among other things, whether and on what terms the claim is settled. A producer who has the contractual right to settle a third-party infringement claim without the writer's consent may settle that claim in ways that are convenient for the production but damaging to the writer, such as making admissions, agreeing to injunctive relief that affects the writer's right to exploit her own work, or paying a settlement that the writer's indemnification obligation will require her to fund. The writer should negotiate for, at minimum, a consent right with respect to any settlement for which her indemnification will be invoked. If the producer wishes to settle a claim over the writer's objection, the producer should bear that cost without recourse to the indemnification clause.

Funding of defense costs raises a related but distinct issue. Even where indemnification is conditioned on a final judgment rather than the mere assertion of a claim, the parties must address who bears the cost of defending the claim while it is pending. A well-negotiated provision will require the parties to cooperate in the defense, allocate interim defense costs proportionally or according to the nature of the claim, and provide for reimbursement if the claim is ultimately resolved in the indemnitor's favor. Writers should also ensure that their indemnification obligation is capped either as a dollar amount or as a percentage of the compensation received under the agreement so that a single meritless but expensive claim does not expose the writer to liability exceeding the total value of the deal.

Force Majeure

Force majeure originates from the French for "superior force" and is the contractual doctrine that excuses a party's non-performance of an obligation when that non-performance is caused by circumstances beyond the party's reasonable control. The doctrine is ancient in origin, rooted in the common law concept of impossibility and the civil law concept of *cas fortuit*, but has maintained modern application from strikes to wars to pandemics. If the agreement does not contain a force majeure clause, the party seeking to invoke the doctrine must rely on the narrower and more demanding common law principles of impossibility or frustration of purpose, which courts apply sparingly.

Force majeure provisions in entertainment contracts allow productions to suspend or terminate agreements when extraordinary events prevent production or, in some cases, development activities from proceeding. The standard list of triggering events in an entertainment force majeure clause typically includes acts of God, war, terrorism, fire, flood, earthquake, epidemic or pandemic, strike or labor disruption, government action, and, in some contracts, "any other cause beyond the party's reasonable control." The force majeure clause can go unnoticed for years until there is an industry or global event that triggers it. In 2020 with the COVID-19 pandemic followed by the 2023 WGA strike, parties scrambled to see what force majeure provision, if any, was in their contracts with it being the most discussed provision for years that followed. In each case, the writers whose agreements contained clear sunset provisions and termination rights fared materially better than those whose agreements did not.

The Suspension Mechanism

The practical effect of a force majeure clause in an entertainment agreement is almost always to suspend the producer's obligations for the duration of the force majeure event, whether that be to shop the project, produce the project, or pay talent on the project. If a production is halted by a guild strike, a pandemic, or a government shutdown order, the producer may invoke force majeure and cease making any payments to the writer that were scheduled during the suspension period. Depending on the agreement, those payments may be deferred until the force majeure period ends and production resumes, or they may be forfeited, depending on how the clause defines the relationship between suspension and termination.

PRO TIP:

In shopping agreements and option agreements, an ill-drafted force majeure clause can extend the period in which the producer has exclusivity over the project for years.

The distinction between suspension and termination is one of the most important in force majeure drafting. A clause that permits the producer to terminate the agreement and thereby extinguish all future payment obligations after a defined suspension period has significant implications for a writer who is mid-development or mid-production when the force majeure event occurs. A writer whose agreement is terminated pursuant to force majeure may lose not only her future milestone payments but also, depending on the termination provisions, any reversionary rights she might otherwise have asserted had the agreement remained in place.

The appropriate negotiating approach for writers is to resist the conflation of suspension and termination. A force majeure clause should suspend the producer's payment obligations for a defined and reasonable period typically no more than six to eight weeks for a production-stage agreement, though market practice varies by project type and budget level and should then give both parties defined rights. If the force majeure event continues beyond the suspension period, the writer should have the right to terminate the agreement and reclaim her rights, not merely to wait indefinitely while the producer's payment obligations remain frozen and the project goes nowhere.

A force majeure clause with no sunset provision that suspends the producer's obligations for as long as the force majeure event continues without giving the writer a right to terminate is functionally equivalent to a reversion provision with no trigger. The producer can invoke it indefinitely, and the writer's project is in limbo for as long as the claimed event persists. The COVID-19 pandemic demonstrated that "as long as the event persists" can mean years. Insist on a defined suspension period and a termination right.

The Scope of Triggering Events

The definition of what constitutes a force majeure event is the other major drafting battleground in this provision. Producers prefer broad, open-ended definitions that include not only classic force majeure events, such as natural disasters, wars, government interdictions, but also economic conditions, financing failures, and market disruptions. Writers should resist the expansion of force majeure to cover events that are, in reality, ordinary business risks that the producer has chosen to accept by entering the agreement. A producer who cannot close financing for a project has not encountered a force majeure event; she has encountered the ordinary risk of the entertainment business. Allowing her to invoke force majeure in response to a financing failure effectively transfers that business risk to the writer, who had no ability to prevent it and no share in the upside that the financing would have generated.

Guild strikes present a related but distinct issue. Most entertainment agreements expressly include labor disputes, strikes, and lockouts in the list of force majeure events, and this is broadly consistent with industry practice. But the inclusion of a guild strike as a force majeure event has implications that writers should understand. If a WGA strike causes the production to suspend, and the force majeure clause permits the producer to suspend the writer's payments without limit, the writer is effectively bearing a portion of the cost of a labor action that the WGA called, in part, to improve the very compensation structures that her agreement embodies. The appropriate qualification is to ensure that the force majeure clause's suspension of payment obligations does not apply to payments that have already been earned, that is, to compensation for services already rendered or milestones already achieved, and that deferred payments accrue interest during any suspension period.

Choice of Law

A choice of law provision is a contractual designation of the governing law that will be used to interpret and enforce the agreement. In the United States, this typically means the designation of a specific state's law. Entertainment agreements almost invariably specify either California or New York law, reflecting the geographic centers of the domestic film and television industry, although that is changing as production grows outside those jurisdictions. The choice of law provision addresses whose law the courts apply in resolving a dispute in the event the parties disagree about what the contract means or requires.

Choice of law matters because contract law is not uniform across jurisdictions. The rules governing contract interpretation, the availability and measure of remedies, the enforceability of specific provisions, and the procedural requirements for asserting or waiving rights all vary meaningfully from state to state. For example, a writer who signs an agreement governed by California law and then brings a breach of contract claim in a New York court will find that the New York court applies California contract principles, which could potentially produce results different from those that would result under New York law.

The practical guidance for writers is to not simply accept a choice of law provision without understanding which jurisdiction it designates, and do not assume that the designated law is neutral. A choice of law provision designating a jurisdiction other than California or New York with no established entertainment law jurisprudence could prove problematic. An agreement governed by, say, Delaware corporate law or Texas contract principles may be interpreted in ways that are inconsistent with established entertainment industry practice, and neither you nor your attorney may be able to predict the outcome of a dispute with confidence.

If you are a California writer working with a California producer on a California-based project, a California choice of law provision is entirely appropriate and familiar. If you are an independent writer in a state with no significant entertainment law infrastructure signing an agreement with a New York-based production company, a New York choice of law provision is not inherently problematic but it does mean that your attorney should be familiar with New York contract principles, and that any future litigation will be conducted under rules you may not fully understand.

PRO TIP:

A sloppy agreement based on a template or a past deal often fails to change the choice of law or governing law to the appropriate state for choice of law or choice of forum. Don't overlook this detail.

Choice of Forum

Writers frequently conflate choice of law with choice of forum as the two are related but distinct provisions. A choice of law clause designates the substantive law that governs the agreement; a forum selection clause (also called a venue clause) designates the specific court or tribunal in which any dispute must be litigated. An agreement may specify California law as the governing law while designating the federal district court for the Southern District of New York as the exclusive forum for litigation. This combination is unusual but not unheard of in multi-jurisdictional entertainment deals.

Forum selection is particularly significant for writers who do not reside in the designated forum. An agreement that requires all disputes to be litigated in Los Angeles Superior Court is functionally manageable for a Los Angeles-based writer but may be economically prohibitive for a writer based in Atlanta, London, or anywhere else that requires travel and the retention of local counsel. The practical lesson is to read the forum selection clause alongside the governing law clause and to evaluate both in terms of their combined effect on your ability to assert your rights if a dispute arises. A favorable governing law is of limited value if the forum in which that law will be applied is inaccessible to you.

Dispute Resolution

A dispute resolution clause establishes the procedural framework within which the parties will resolve disagreements that cannot be settled informally. In entertainment agreements, dispute resolution provisions typically present a binary choice: the parties will litigate their disputes in a court of competent jurisdiction, or they will use alternative dispute resolution (ADR) options, specifically arbitration and/or mediation. A growing number of agreements require the parties to attempt mediation before proceeding to either litigation or arbitration that is cost-effective and favorable to writers as discussed below.

The choice between litigation and arbitration has substantive consequences that affect the writer's practical ability to assert her rights and the likely outcome of any dispute. Writers entering agreements containing arbitration clauses should understand those consequences clearly, because arbitration clauses are routinely presented as standard boilerplate. Courts have consistently enforced them, with limited exceptions, regardless of whether the signing party fully understood their implications.

Arbitration

Arbitration is a private adjudicatory process in which the parties' dispute is submitted to one or more arbitrators whose decision is binding on the parties and, with narrow exceptions, not subject to appellate review. Arbitrators are private individuals, typically attorneys or retired judges with subject matter expertise. The advantages of arbitration over litigation benefit both parties in that it is faster than court litigation; it is private, conducted outside the public court record;

it is conducted before a decision-maker with industry expertise rather than a generalist judge; and it avoids the uncertainty and expense of jury selection in complex commercial cases; it saves significant attorney fees necessary for a litigated court case.

The disadvantages of arbitration are equally real. The most significant is the near-total absence of appellate review. A court judgment can be appealed on grounds of legal error; an arbitration award can be vacated only on very narrow grounds, such as fraud, corruption, disregard of the law, that courts interpret restrictively. This means that an arbitrator who reaches a legally incorrect conclusion has, in practical effect, the last word. A writer who loses an arbitration on a legal theory that is incorrect may have no meaningful avenue for correcting the error.

While the cost of court litigation is expensive, arbitration is not without its expense. Arbitration requires the parties to fund the arbitrator's fees which can run to several hundred dollars per hour, with major arbitrations generating arbitrator billings of tens or hundreds of thousands of dollars, in addition to their own attorneys' fees. In a dispute between a writer and a well-resourced studio or production company, the cost of arbitration may effectively price the writer out of the process, even when her legal position is strong.

Writers should also attend to the specific arbitral rules designated in the arbitration clause. The two most common sets of rules in entertainment industry arbitration are those of JAMS (formerly Judicial Arbitration and Mediation Services) and the American Arbitration Association (AAA). Both organizations offer different rule sets for commercial disputes of different sizes, and the applicable rules determine, among other things, the number of arbitrators, the discovery procedures available to the parties, the timeline for the proceeding, and the allocation of arbitration costs. A clause that simply requires "arbitration" without specifying the applicable rules, the number of arbitrators, or the seat of the arbitration has left critical procedural questions unresolved that will be answered either by negotiation at the time of the dispute or by the arbitral tribunal itself, neither of which is an ideal position to be in.

Mediation

Mediation is a non-binding, facilitated negotiation process in which a neutral third party, the mediator, assists the parties in reaching a voluntary resolution of their dispute. Unlike arbitration, mediation does not produce a binding decision; the mediator has no authority to impose an outcome. The process succeeds only when both parties agree to a resolution, which means that either party retains the ability to walk away. This non-binding character is precisely what makes mediation valuable as a first step in a dispute resolution framework: it preserves the parties' options while creating a structured opportunity to resolve the dispute without the cost and adversarial escalation of formal proceedings.

Entertainment agreements sometimes require mediation before arbitration or litigation is permitted. However, the devil is in the details: how long are the parties required to mediate before either may proceed to arbitration or litigation; who bears the cost of mediation (typically split equally); and whether the mediation requirement can be bypassed in emergency situations where immediate relief is necessary. A mediation first clause that requires a sixty-day mediation period before a party may seek emergency injunctive relief is not a sensible provision; one that requires a thirty-day good-faith mediation effort before commencing a standard commercial arbitration is entirely workable.

The practical value of mediation in entertainment disputes is often underappreciated, because the disputes that make news and establish precedent proceeded all the way through litigation or arbitration. The disputes that resolved quietly in mediation are invisible in the public record, but they are far more numerous. A well-conducted mediation, before adversarial positions have calcified and legal fees have accumulated, is frequently the most efficient and least damaging pathway to resolution for both parties. Writers should not reflexively resist mediation requirements; they should ensure that the mediation clause is sensibly drafted and that the timeline for completing mediation before proceeding to formal dispute resolution is reasonable.

Injunctive Relief Waiver

Another boilerplate provision to be aware of is the injunctive relief waiver by which a party agrees in advance not to seek a court order stopping the producer from proceeding with the project, or with the exploitation of the project, regardless of the nature or severity of the producer's alleged breach. In other words, the only remedy in the event of a breach is monetary damages. While that might seem like a bad thing, if a derivative of your script is being used without your approval and getting ready to be distributed worldwide.

Studios and producers insist on this waiver because the financial stakes of a film or television production are too great to be subject to the risk that a single contributor, say a writer, a director, a performer, could halt the release of a project worth tens or hundreds of millions of dollars by obtaining an injunction over a contract dispute. From the producer's perspective, money damages are an adequate remedy for any wrong the writer is likely to suffer; the project itself, once underway, must be permitted to proceed.

The practical effect of the waiver is significant. Without injunctive relief, the writer cannot stop a producer from releasing a film that has been altered in ways the writer believes violate the agreement, from crediting another writer on material the writer believes she alone authored, or from exploiting rights the writer believes were never properly conveyed. The writer's only recourse is to sue for damages after the fact, which means proving in court the dollar value of a harm that may be difficult or impossible to quantify. The damage to a writer's reputation from being miscredited, the loss of creative integrity from an unauthorized alteration, the lost future opportunities from a botched first production of her work may not cleanly translate into a monetary damages calculation.

Writers should approach the injunctive relief waiver with realism. In a major studio or streaming deal, the waiver is non-negotiable as a matter of standard practice, and refusing to sign it will almost certainly end the deal. The most a writer can typically achieve at that level is a carve-out preserving injunctive relief for specific, narrowly defined breaches, most commonly, the producer's failure to pay sums due, breach of confidentiality obligations regarding the writer's pre-production materials, or unauthorized use of the writer's name or likeness in marketing.

In independent film and lower-budget television, where the leverage differential is less extreme, broader carve-outs may be achievable, including for material breaches of the credit provisions or for exploitation of rights expressly reserved to the writer. The objective is not to eliminate the waiver, which is unrealistic, but to identify the categories of breach for which money damages would be plainly inadequate and to preserve the equitable remedy in those specific cases.

Class Action Waivers

Some entertainment agreements, particularly those used by larger studios and streaming platforms in agreements with independent writers, include provisions waiving the writer's right to participate in any class action, collective action, or representative proceeding arising from the agreement. These waivers, when combined with a mandatory arbitration clause, effectively require the writer to resolve any dispute individually foreclosing the possibility of joining with other similarly situated writers to challenge systemic contract practices.

Class action waivers are controversial in consumer and employment contexts, and their enforceability has been the subject of significant litigation. In the commercial context of an arms-length entertainment agreement, they are generally enforceable under federal arbitration law, as interpreted by the Supreme Court in a line of cases beginning with *AT&T Mobility v. Concepcion*. For a dispute about the specific terms of a specific agreement, the class action waiver is irrelevant as such disputes are inherently individual. However, for a dispute that implicates practices applied across a large number of similarly situated writers, such as systematic underpayment of backend, or systematic misclassification of material as non-qualifying for separated rights purposes, the class action waiver removes a potentially powerful tool for collective redress.

Writers should not assume that a class action waiver is either standard or harmless. They should read it, understand what it forecloses, and at minimum ensure that their attorney has explained its implications before the agreement is signed.

What the Fine Print Actually Does

The provisions addressed in this chapter only activate when something goes wrong. This is exactly why they may not have been tested in previous transactions. That doesn't exclude the possibility of something going wrong, for example, a third party sues, a catastrophe shuts down production, or the parties can't agree and are forced into adversarial proceedings. Because they are contingent, they feel theoretical at the moment of signing. However, they are the legal framework that governs the relationship between the writer and the producer in every scenario in which that relationship becomes difficult, contested, or hostile.

The discipline of reading boilerplate as a dealmaker rather than as a writer eager to close a deal and move into production requires a specific mental shift. It requires asking not "what are we agreeing to?" but "what happens when this agreement breaks down?" Who pays if a copyright claim is filed? Who has the right to settle it? What happens to the project if a pandemic shuts down the industry for eighteen months? Under whose legal system will a dispute about the reversion trigger be resolved, and in whose courthouse? If the arbitrator gets it wrong, does the writer have any recourse? Though contemplating these issues may seem pessimistic, they are nonetheless a matter of professional routine. These are also issues at which most agents or managers are not adept. Developing the capacity to be aware of and ask those questions is the role of a professional dealmaker.

The final chapter that follows completes the vocabulary you will need to operate in this industry, including the common deal terms, profit definitions, and industry language that appear in agreements, in pitch meetings, and in conversations with your professional representatives.

CHAPTER 15

SPEAKING THE INDUSTRY LANGUAGE

The language of the entertainment industry has developed organically over decades of deal-making, accumulated guild agreements, and industry custom. While it might seem like everyday lingo to industry professionals, it's not common language used in business, nor in other areas of law. Although I had been a practicing attorney for decades, learning the language used in the entertainment industry was a completely new skill set that came with experience. This is the primary reason I wanted to write this book—so that you can fast track the process to learning the business side of the industry.

Throughout the book, you've been introduced to much of the industry lingo. This chapter attempts to summarize and fill in the gaps to address the terms that appear most frequently in the agreements and conversations that creators encounter at each stage of a project's life. These terms carry legal and economic weight, and are also susceptible to being misunderstood, misapplied, or strategically obscured by the party with the superior bargaining position. Understanding these terms is not a substitute for legal counsel, but it is a prerequisite for having a productive conversation with legal counsel and for recognizing when the language of an agreement is drifting away from the deal you thought you made.

The terms below are presented not as an alphabetical glossary but in the logical sequence in which they tend to appear in the life of a project. Some of the terms have been covered elsewhere in the book but are included here for review and quick reference. To that end, the chapter is organized in three sections. The first addresses common deal terms encountered in film and television transactions. The second addresses the profit definitions that determine how and whether a writer participates in the financial success of a produced project. The third addresses the development-to-production stages through which a project typically moves from initial acquisition to greenlight. Taken together, these three sections complete the vocabulary framework that the preceding chapters have been building.

Rights and Acquisition Terms

Assignment—A complete transfer of a party's rights under an agreement, or of the underlying intellectual property itself, to a third party. Assignments can be contractual wherein a producer assigns her development agreement to a studio, or they can be copyright assignments, in which the ownership of the copyright itself passes from the assignor to the assignee. Under 17 U.S.C. § 204(a), a copyright assignment must be in writing and signed by the assignor; an oral assignment of copyright is unenforceable.

Separate from the type of assignment described above, an *assignment clause* in the boilerplate of an agreement is common and allows or disallows the parties to assign the actual agreement itself. Oftentimes, the writer is prohibited to assign the agreement, but the producer is granted the right. However, writers should ensure that any agreement granting a producer the right to assign the agreement to a third party without the writer's consent contains, at minimum, a condition that the assignee assumes all of the producer's obligations to the writer under the original agreement.

Option—A contractual right, obtained for a fixed consideration, to purchase specified rights within a defined period on pre-negotiated terms. The option itself conveys no ownership of the underlying rights; it conveys only the exclusive right to decide whether to purchase the rights. During the option period, the producer may develop the project, seek financing, and attach talent, but the writer retains ownership of the material unless and until the option is exercised. The option price may or may not be applied against the purchase price if the option is exercised.

Most Favored Nations—A most favored nations (MFN) provision is a contractual guarantee that one party will receive treatment no less favorable than that given to a designated comparator on a specified deal point. In entertainment agreements, MFN clauses most often attach to compensation, credit, perks (travel, accommodations, dressing rooms), or backend participation, and they typically arise when multiple talent or rights holders are being assembled around a single project. If a writer negotiates an MFN on credit position with the other credited writers on the project, then any improvement in another writer's credit must be matched for the MFN beneficiary. The practical effect is that the producer cannot quietly give a better deal to a comparable participant without automatically improving the MFN beneficiary's deal as well.

Purchase Price—The consideration paid by the producer to the writer in exchange for the conveyance of the specified rights. In an option-purchase agreement, the purchase price is the amount paid at the time the option is exercised, typically reduced by the option consideration already paid. Purchase prices in literary acquisition deals are often expressed as a percentage of the production budget, subject to a negotiated floor and/or ceiling, that ties the writer's compensation to the scale of the production while providing minimum and maximum guarantees.

Separated Rights—A category of rights that certain qualifying writers retain in their original material even after that material has been acquired by a studio or producer under a WGA-covered agreement. Separated rights include, among others, the right to publish a novelization of the screenplay, the right to produce a stage adaptation, and certain sequel and spin-off participation rights. Separated rights are not automatic; they are determined by the WGA's credit arbitration process, and a writer must have performed a specified minimum of original work on the project to qualify. Writers who are not covered by a WGA agreement do not receive separated rights as a matter of guild rule and therefore must negotiate comparable protections contractually.

Shopping Agreement—An agreement, typically exclusive, authorizing a producer to pitch the writer's project to potential buyers, studios, networks, streaming platforms, or financiers without acquiring an option on the underlying rights. Shopping agreements are the most informal entry point in the acquisition spectrum. The writer or rightsholder may negotiate to retain the right to pitch the project themselves or through other representatives during the shopping period. The critical drafting concern is ensuring that the shopping period has a defined and reasonable end date, after which the producer's authority to shop the project lapses without continued attachment.

Underlying Rights—The intellectual property rights in the source material upon which a screenplay, teleplay, or other production is based. When a producer acquires underlying rights, she acquires the right to use the protected elements of the source material, which includes the characters, plot, dialogue, and narrative structure, as the basis for a new work. As discussed previously, a project built on uncleared underlying rights has a potentially fatal chain of title defect.

Work Made for Hire—A legal characterization in which the hiring party, rather than the individual who created the work, is deemed the author for copyright purposes from the moment of creation. In the entertainment context, work-for-hire agreements are used when a producer hires or employs a writer to write or rewrite a screenplay to the producer's specifications. The writer receives compensation for her services but retains no copyright interest in the resulting work.

The distinction between a work-for-hire engagement and an acquisition of an original work matters because the rights package, the credit structure, and the writer's residual entitlements are all different. Writers who are engaged on a work-for-hire basis for rewrite or polish services should understand that they are selling labor, not rights, and thus the compensation they receive should reflect that distinction.

Deal Structure and Economic Terms

Attachment—The formal association of a creative party, usually a writer, director, producer, or actor, with a project memorialized in a letter of intent, deal memo, or fully executed agreement. An attachment signals to the marketplace that the attached party has committed to the project, which may increase its salability or facilitate financing. Attachments carry legal implications in that an attached writer who has executed an agreement may be entitled to compensation if the project proceeds without her, and a producer with an attachment agreement may be entitled to a producing credit and fee regardless of her actual contribution to the production. Writers who are asked to attach themselves to a project, particularly in exchange for speculative compensation, should ensure that the attachment agreement clearly defines what the attachment entitles them to receive.

First Look Deal—An agreement under which a writer or producer is obligated to offer her next project, or projects developed during a defined period, to a specific studio or network before taking them elsewhere. First look deals are typically accompanied by a development fund and an overhead payment, making them attractive to writers who want institutional support for their work. The trade-off is exclusivity. During the first look period, the writer cannot freely shop new projects to other buyers until the first look partner has had a defined opportunity to pass. Writers in first look deals should pay careful attention to the definition of what projects are subject to the first look obligation and what constitutes a timely pass by the first look partner.

Pay or Play—A contractual commitment by the producer to pay the writer (or talent) her full agreed compensation regardless of whether the writer's services are ultimately used or whether the production proceeds. A pay-or-play commitment converts the producer's payment obligation from a contingency into an unconditional one. Pay-or-play protections are typically reserved for established writers with significant negotiating leverage, but the concept is relevant to any writer who has committed time, opportunity cost, and creative energy to a project. The question becomes whether the compensation she is to receive is conditional on outcomes she cannot control, or whether it is guaranteed regardless of the producer's subsequent decisions.

Overall Deal—A more comprehensive arrangement, typically in television, under which a writer is placed exclusively at a network or studio for a defined period, receives a guaranteed fee, and develops projects in partnership with the institution. Overall deals are the top of the television writer market and represent the studio's bet on a writer's consistent ability to generate commercially viable material. For the writer, the appeal is financial security and institutional resources; the constraint is exclusivity and the obligation to develop primarily within the institution's priorities. The negotiation of an overall deal involves most of the deal point categories addressed in this book, compressed into a single, long-term commercial relationship.

Step Deal—A writing agreement structured as a series of sequential steps—typically treatment, first draft, revision, and polish—in which the producer has the right, but not the obligation, to proceed to each successive step. The writer is paid for each completed step; the producer's decision not to proceed to a subsequent step terminates the agreement without further payment obligation. Step deals are the standard structure for screenwriting service agreements in the studio context. Writers entering step deals should understand that the producer's right to stop the engagement at any step is a feature of the structure, not a breach of the agreement, and should negotiate accordingly particularly with respect to the compensation at each step and the rights retained if the deal is terminated before final delivery.

Turnaround—The right of a writer or rightsholder to reclaim a project that the acquiring party has declined to produce. As discussed in Chapter 13, the turnaround right is conditioned on reimbursement of the development costs the acquiring party has incurred, including in most cases the original acquisition price plus some portion of development expenditures. Turnaround rights are among the most practically important provisions for writers in long-term development relationships, and the terms governing the turnaround price are among the most consequential in any acquisition agreement.

Profit Definitions

The vocabulary governing profit participation contains some of the most obscure terms in the entertainment industry. A writer who negotiates backend participation in a film or television project without understanding precisely what the agreement means by "gross receipts," "net profits," "adjusted gross," or "defined proceeds" may be in for an unpleasant surprise. The profit definitions used by major studios and production companies are the product of decades of accumulated accounting practice, guild negotiation, and contractual evolution. The terms are generally used internally and practically effective at ensuring that projects which generate a generous amount of money for their distributors and financiers nonetheless show little or no profit on the books. Understanding how that happens requires understanding the basic terms used.

Gross Receipts

Gross receipts, sometimes called gross revenues or simply "gross," refers to the total amount of money received by the distributing entity from the exploitation of a film, book, or television project across all media and territories, before any deductions are taken. In theory, gross receipts is the broadest and most favorable profit base from which a participant can receive a share—and also the rarest. A writer who negotiates a percentage of gross receipts is entitled to be paid from the first dollar received, before the studio takes its distribution fee, before production costs are recouped, and before any of the deductions that define the net profit calculation are applied.

In practice, gross participations are almost never negotiated by writers, even experienced and commercially successful ones. They are the province of above-the-line talent with extraordinary market leverage or the director whose attachment is a condition of financing. For everyone else, gross participation in its pure form is a theoretical concept rather than a practical negotiating outcome.

Distribution Fees

The first and most significant deduction from gross receipts in virtually every profit definition is the distribution fee, which is a percentage of gross receipts retained by the distributor as compensation for its distribution services. Distribution fees are charged on top of the actual distribution expenses, which are separately deducted. The distribution fee is, in economic terms, the distributor's profit margin, taken off the top before any other participant sees a dollar.

Distribution fees vary by medium and territory, and the specific percentages are negotiated or, in most guild and standard agreements, set by industry convention. Theatrical distribution fees charged by major studios have historically ranged from thirty to forty percent of theatrical gross receipts in North America, with higher fees in some foreign territories where the distribution infrastructure is more expensive to maintain. Television license fees, streaming distribution fees, and home video distribution fees are calculated differently and may be subject to different percentage structures, all of which are specified in the distribution fee schedule attached to or incorporated into the profit definition.

Distribution Expenses

After the distribution fee is deducted, distribution expenses are deducted from what remains. Distribution expenses include the actual costs of bringing the project to market, including prints and advertising (P&A) for theatrical releases, which can run to tens of millions of dollars for a wide release; residuals and guild obligations paid to talent and crew; taxes and duties in foreign territories; and the various other costs associated with releasing a film or series across multiple platforms and markets. These are hard costs and their effect on the net profit calculation is substantial. A theatrical film with a fifty-million-dollar marketing campaign has incurred fifty million dollars in distribution expenses that must be fully recouped before net profits can begin to accrue.

Production Costs and the Break-Even

After distribution fees and distribution expenses are deducted, the production cost of the film itself is deducted from whatever remains. Production cost, or the negative cost, includes not only the direct cost of making the film (cast fees, crew wages, locations, sets, visual effects, and post-production) but also, in studio accounting, an overhead charge that is typically fifteen to twenty percent added to the production budget to compensate the studio for its administrative and institutional infrastructure. This overhead charge is an accounting allocation that increases the production cost figure and therefore the amount that must be recouped before net profits.

The combined effect of the distribution fee, distribution expenses, negative cost, and overhead charge is that a project must generate gross receipts substantially in excess of its production budget before it reaches the break-even point at which revenues equal deducted costs and therefore before any net profit participant receives anything. In practice, it is the line producer who prepares and manages the production budget against which these deductions are measured, tracking every line item of negative cost from pre-production through post. Because that budget becomes the negative cost figure in the net profit waterfall, the line producer's accounting decisions, what gets allocated where, what is capitalized into the production budget versus charged elsewhere, materially shape the number that net profit participants are eventually measured against.

For example, a film with a one-hundred-million-dollar negative cost, a fifteen-million-dollar overhead charge, a fifty-million-dollar P&A budget, and a thirty-five-percent distribution fee must generate approximately two hundred and fifty million dollars in global gross receipts before it technically breaks even under a standard studio net profit definition. Many films that are commercially considered successful generating significant box office revenue and celebrated as franchise properties may never reach that break-even point on the books, and their net profit participants receive nothing.

Adjusted Gross and Defined Proceeds

Between the extremes of first-dollar gross participation and standard net profits, the industry has developed a range of intermediate profit definitions that are more favorable than net profits but less favorable than pure gross. These intermediate definitions go by various names with adjusted gross, modified gross, defined proceeds, and enhanced gross among the most common. They share a common structure in that they begin with gross receipts and deduct a more limited set of items than a standard net profit definition would, resulting in a larger base from which the participant's share is calculated.

The specific content of an adjusted gross or defined proceeds definition varies significantly from agreement to agreement, and the label alone tells you almost nothing. An "adjusted gross" definition that deducts distribution fees, distribution expenses, and residuals but not production costs or overhead is meaningfully more favorable than a net profit definition. An "adjusted gross" definition that deducts all of those items plus a different set of overhead charges under a different label has accomplished very little by changing the name. The operative question, as with every provision addressed in this book, is not what the definition is called but what it actually permits to be deducted and in what order.

When reviewing a profit definition, it's important to identify every deduction, quantify its likely effect given the economics of the specific project, and compare the result to market practice for writers at your level of the market. The definition adopted by the production is rarely, if ever, changeable and thus it is about negotiating the percentage being proposed in the agreement, or else adjusting your own expectations for what you are likely to receive down the road.

Audit Rights

A writer who has negotiated any form of backend participation should also negotiate what's known as an audit right. This is the contractual entitlement to examine the producing and distributing entity's books and records to verify that the profit statements it has provided are accurate and complete. Audit rights are standard in guild agreements and are available in most non-guild agreements to writers with the leverage to insist on them. They can be, however, expensive to exercise. A full audit of a studio's accounting records for a major release requires the engagement of a specialized entertainment accountant and may cost tens of thousands of dollars. They are also the only mechanism by which a profit participant can independently verify the accuracy of what she has been told she is owed.

Audit findings in major entertainment accounting disputes have historically revealed underpayments ranging from clerical errors to systematic misapplication of the applicable profit definitions. The existence of an audit right does not guarantee that the writer will be paid correctly; it guarantees only that she has a contractual basis for investigating whether she has been paid correctly and for asserting a claim if she has not. Without an audit right, the writer is entirely dependent on the accuracy of accounting statements prepared by the party with a financial interest in minimizing what those statements show.

Development Phase

Development, in the entertainment industry, refers to the process by which a project is brought from initial concept or acquisition to the point of a greenlight. Development encompasses the acquisition of underlying rights, the commissioning of successive screenplay drafts, the attachment of key creative elements, the pursuit of financing, and the various pitch and packaging activities that are intended to build the project's commercial viability to the threshold at which a studio, network, or financier commits to fund production. Development is, in other words, everything that happens to a project before it is actually made and the phase in which the topics in this book are most applicable.

A project in development has no guarantee of production. The writer may spend months or years in active development on a project revising drafts, participating in meetings, providing notes only to have the project stalled, shelved, or abandoned when the producer cannot secure financing or when the studio loses interest. The compensation paid during development in the form of option payments, step deal fees, and development drafts fees is payment for services rendered and rights conveyed, not an advance against production compensation. If the project does not proceed to production, the writer does not receive her production bonus, her screen credit, or any of the backend participation that was contingent on production.

Development also has a specific legal significance with respect to the copyright in successive drafts. Each draft of a screenplay delivered during the development process is a new work, or a derivative work based on the prior draft, and the question of who owns the copyright in each draft and in the collective development work product is governed by the terms of the applicable agreement. A writer engaged on a work-for-hire basis owns nothing she has created during development. A writer who has conveyed rights by assignment owns nothing after the assignment. A writer who has retained copyright subject to a license or an option may own the drafts but may be constrained in her ability to exploit them independently. The ownership of development drafts determines what the writer can do with the material if the project does not proceed to production.

The Development Deal

The term "development deal" is used loosely in the industry to describe any arrangement under which a producing entity commits resources, typically a combination of a writing fee and an overhead or production support budget, to developing a project with a writer over a defined period. Development deals range in scope from a modest option-plus-one-draft arrangement to a multi-year, multi-project commitment structured as a first look or overall deal.

The legal question becomes what the producing entity receives in exchange for its development investment, and what the writer retains if the development investment does not result in a production commitment. A producing entity that funds three drafts of a screenplay and then declines to greenlight the project has not necessarily lost its investment; depending on the agreement, it may retain the right to continue exploiting the development work product, to shop the project to other buyers, or to hold the underlying rights while the project sits in turnaround. The writer's ability to extricate herself from that situation and reclaim her material and take it elsewhere depends entirely on the reversion and turnaround provisions she negotiated before the development process began.

This is why the boilerplate provisions addressed in Chapter 14 and the long-term deal points addressed in Chapter 13 are crucial to the development deal. A development deal without a reversion trigger is not a development deal with an incomplete provision; instead, it is a development deal in which the producing entity has the right to hold the writer's material indefinitely, whether or not development is proceeding.

The Production Phase

Production, in the legal and contractual sense, is the phase of a project's life that begins with a formal commitment to fund and make the project and ends with the delivery of the completed work to the distributing or exhibiting entity. The transition from development to production is triggered by a "greenlight" and is typically memorialized through the execution of production agreements with key creative elements, the opening of a production account, and the commencement of pre-production activities.

The legal significance of the development-to-production transition is substantial. Many of the payment obligations that arise under a writer's agreement, such as the production bonus, the screen credit determination process, the commencement of backend participation accrual, and the activation of certain guild protections are conditioned on the project reaching production. A project that is greenlighted but does not commence principal photography within a defined period may trigger reversion provisions; whereas a project that commences principal photography satisfies those triggers and extinguishes the writer's right to reclaim her material. The precise definition of "commencement of principal photography" therefore becomes consequential as discussed in Chapter 13.

In television, the development-to-production continuum is more granular than in film. A television project typically moves through several intermediate stages—script commitment, pilot order, series order—each of which represents an incremental production commitment with its own payment obligations, creative deliverables, and legal implications. A script commitment funds the writing of a pilot script without committing to produce the pilot; a pilot order commits to the production of a single pilot episode; a series order commits to a defined number of episodes of the full series. Writers in television must understand where they are in this continuum at every stage of a negotiation, because the compensation, credit, and rights implications are different at each step.

Development Hell

"Development hell" is the industry's colloquial term for the condition in which a project has been in active or nominal development for an extended period without reaching a production commitment. A project in development hell is a project whose underlying rights are encumbered, whose writer cannot freely take the material elsewhere, and whose commercial potential is eroding as the marketplace moves on to newer material and more current cultural reference points. A deal memo or short-form agreement that describes a project as being "in development" without specifying what development milestones the producer is obligated to achieve, and by when, is an agreement that provides the producer with the maximum possible flexibility to hold the project without advancing it. Vague development language benefits the party with control of the rights, which, once the agreement is signed, is not the writer or rightsholder.

Development hell can result when an option period that has been extended multiple times through timely payment of extension fees, a shopping agreement that has not technically lapsed because the producer continues to pay nominal fees, or a purchase agreement in which the reversion trigger has been carefully drafted to give the producer maximum flexibility to maintain control without advancing the project. In each case, the project is stalled and the writer's ability to extract herself from the situation depends on whether she negotiated the provisions that would give her that right.

The chapter that follows from here takes this vocabulary and applies it to the final dimensions of a writer's professional life including the long-term management of her intellectual property portfolio, the relationships with representatives that will shape the trajectory of her career, and the discipline of thinking about her creative work not only as artistic expression but as a body of assets that require care, documentation, and strategic management over the full span of a professional lifetime.

FINAL SCENE

BUILDING A SUSTAINABLE CAREER

Act II introduced the distinction between the creative and the dealmaker. The creative writes from instinct, empathy, and attachment. The dealmaker assesses value, identifies risk, and negotiates with objectivity. Contrary to what some might think, the dealmaker's perspective does not diminish the creative; it protects and builds a sustainable career. Writers need both capacities.

Thinking like a businessperson does not mean becoming transactional in your creative work. It does not mean writing to market, optimizing for commercial appeal at the expense of artistic integrity, or viewing your collaborators primarily as adversaries. It means understanding that the creative work you produce has commercial value and that other parties in the entertainment ecosystem have a financial interest in acquiring that value on the most favorable terms available to them.

Knowing Your Value at Every Stage

A writer who thinks like a businessperson evaluates her work relative to what comparable writers with comparable credits are receiving for comparable material in comparable transactions. That knowledge is not always easy to obtain because the entertainment industry does not publish a price list and because compensation information is often treated as confidential by the parties who have it. But it is obtainable, through representation, through guild resources, through professional networks, and through the kind of relationship with a knowledgeable entertainment attorney.

Knowing your value means understanding how your leverage changes at different stages of a project's development. How the value of an un-optioned screenplay differs from the value of a screenplay with a producer attachment, and how both differ from the value of a screenplay for which two studios are actively competing. It means understanding how your professional credits affect your negotiating position, and how a single high-profile produced credit can shift the entire landscape of what you can demand and receive.

Managing Your Portfolio of Work

A businessperson manages a portfolio of assets with different risk profiles, different liquidity characteristics, and different long-term value trajectories. A writer who thinks like a businessperson does the same thing with her creative work. Not every project in the portfolio will be produced. Not every produced project will succeed commercially. Not every commercially successful project will generate backend participation. But a writer with a well-managed portfolio of projects—some optioned, some in development, some produced, some held—is in a stronger position than a writer whose entire professional identity and economic security rests on a single project in a single producer's hands.

Portfolio management for writers may entail not optioning everything you write to the first producer who expresses interest knowing that an optioned script is an encumbered asset that you cannot freely develop or sell elsewhere during the option period. It means maintaining a clear, documented record of what rights you hold, what rights you have conveyed, to whom, under what terms, and when those terms expire. It means understanding which of your projects have the broadest commercial potential and protecting those most carefully, while being more flexible about projects where the commercial stakes are lower. And it means understanding that the rights in a produced work may generate value for decades, and that the agreements you sign today will govern that value for the full duration of copyright protection, which under current law extends for the life of the author plus seventy years.

Building and Maintaining Professional Relationships

Thinking like a businessperson also means understanding the role that professional relationships play in a long career and managing those relationships with the same intentionality that you bring to managing your agreements. You will hear over and over that the entertainment industry is a relationship business. Projects get made because the right people know each other, trust each other, and have track records of productive collaboration. A writer who is difficult to work with, unreliable in her professional commitments, or careless about the professional reputations of her collaborators will find that her creative talent is insufficient compensation for the friction she introduces into the production process.

At the same time, thinking like a businessperson means recognizing that professional warmth is not a substitute for documented agreements. The producers, directors, and studio executives with whom you build genuine and productive creative relationships are counterparties and the agreements that govern your relationship with them will outlast the goodwill originally expressed. The writers who build the longest and most productive careers in the entertainment industry are those who are simultaneously excellent collaborators and professionals who bring warmth and creative generosity to their relationships, along with legal literacy to the agreements that govern those relationships.

Protecting Your Intellectual Property Over Time

The opening chapters of this book introduced copyright as the legal foundation on which every other provision in an entertainment agreement rests. Copyright is the right that makes your screenplay valuable to a producer, your novel valuable to a studio, your original characters valuable to a franchise builder. It is the right that gives you something to negotiate with, to option, sell, license, or retain. Protecting that foundation over the course of a long career is a practice that ensures that your copyright interests remain clear, documented, and defensible at every stage of your professional life.

The copyright registration chapter of this book made the legal case for timely registration in detail: the availability of statutory damages and attorneys' fees for infringement that occurs after registration; the establishment of a public record of ownership and date of creation; the procedural advantages that registration provides in any subsequent dispute. Timely registration means registration within three months of first publication or, for unpublished works, registration before any significant distribution of the work to third parties. It means registering each draft that constitutes a meaningful creative departure from the prior version, not merely the final produced version. It means maintaining a registration log of your own to evidence the registration rather than requiring a search of archives that may have been incompletely maintained.

Similarly, it's important to maintain your own chain of title by documenting how copyright ownership has passed from the original author to each successive owner or licensee. A creative who spends twenty years in the entertainment industry will generate dozens of agreements, dozens of rights transfers, dozens of option grants and license agreements and work-for-hire engagements. Each of those transactions is a link in the chain of title for some work, and each link must be properly executed, properly documented, and properly retained if the chain is to remain clean. A writer who cannot produce the executed agreement governing a rights transfer that occurred fifteen years ago has a chain of title problem that may cloud not only that work but every work that has been developed from it since.

It's important to store every executed agreement in a secure, organized, and accessible archive, physical or digital or both. Every option extension, amendment, or modification to a prior agreement must be documented in writing and added to the relevant file. Don't solely rely on your representative to do it for you. People die, lose documents in natural disasters, or loosely keep their own computer files.

Tracking the Termination Right

The statutory termination right under Section 203 of Title 17 was introduced earlier in the context of reversion and deserves a fuller treatment here, in the context of a career's long arc, because it represents one of the most underutilized protections that copyright law affords to authors who have made grants of their rights. Professionals and artists in the music industry rely on this statutory right for ownership of their works.

Section 203 permits authors and, after the author's death, specified statutory heirs to terminate grants of copyright made on or after January 1, 1978, during a five-year window that opens thirty-five years after the date of the grant. The termination right is non-waivable, regardless of what the agreement says, and its exercise cannot be conditioned on the payment of any additional consideration. A writer who assigned her copyright in a screenplay in 1990 for a purchase price that now looks grossly inadequate, given the franchise value the work has generated, has the right to reclaim that copyright and to renegotiate with the current rights holder from a position of legal entitlement beginning in 2025.

The procedural requirements for exercising the termination right are specific: notice must be served no earlier than ten years and no later than two years before the effective date of termination, and the notice must comply with the formal requirements specified in the Copyright Office's regulations. A writer who misses the notice window loses the right to terminate during that five-year window entirely, though she may have another opportunity if the grant covered rights that began to run from a later date.

For writers early in their careers who are signing agreements today, the termination right may feel remote, after all it's three and a half decades away. However, the agreements you sign today will still be governing the exploitation of your work when the termination window opens. The franchise built on your original screenplay may be generating its third remake and its seventh spin-off by then. The termination right may be the most significant single piece of legal leverage available to you. This is further reason to keep adequate records to track when the window approaches.

Fair Use, Public Domain, and Emerging Rights

Protecting your intellectual property over time also means remaining attentive to changes in the legal and commercial landscape that affect the value and enforceability of your rights. The copyright law that governs your work today is not static. Congress has amended the Copyright Act multiple times since its major revision in 1976, and the courts continue to interpret its provisions in ways that affect the scope of protection available to authors. The fair use doctrine, whose limitations were examined in detail earlier in this book, is litigated continuously, and the boundaries of what constitutes permissible use of an author's work shift with each significant appellate decision. A writer who is producing work that others are likely to want to adapt, sample, or build upon or, vice versa, who is herself adapting, sampling, or building upon the work of others has a continuing interest in understanding how those boundaries are evolving.

The expansion of the public domain is another dimension of the landscape that writers benefit from monitoring. As of 2026, works published before January 1, 1928, are now in the public domain in the United States, and the public domain expands each January 1st as additional works whose copyright terms have expired become freely available for adaptation without licensing. A writer who understands which source materials are in the public domain and which remain protected can make informed decisions about underlying rights clearance and can sometimes identify adaptation opportunities.

Finally, the emergence of artificial intelligence as a tool for generating creative content raises intellectual property questions that are, at the time of this writing, actively litigated and far from resolved. The extent to which AI-generated content is protectable under copyright law, the extent to which AI training on copyrighted works constitutes infringement, and the implications of AI-generated screenplays and story treatments for writers' rights and compensation are questions that will shape the landscape of the entertainment industry in the years ahead. Writers who stay up to date with these evolving issues have a better understanding of what legal protections are available to them.

Forming a Legal Entity

At some point in the development of a creative career, a writer or other creative will encounter the question of whether to operate as a sole proprietor or to form a legal entity, most commonly a limited liability company (LLC), through which to conduct her professional activities. The decision should be approached from the perspective of legalities, tax consequences, and that of professional optics. The right answer depends on the specific circumstances of the writer's career, income, risk profile, and the kinds of projects she is taking on.

There are several reasons a creative might choose to form an LLC or other entity. The first is liability protection. An LLC, properly formed and properly maintained, creates a legal separation between the writer's personal assets and the business activities of the entity. If a project produced through the LLC gives rise to a lawsuit, such as a claim of infringement, a contract dispute, an accusation that the work defamed a real person, then the writer's personal home, savings, and other assets are, in most circumstances, shielded from that liability. The same writer operating in her own name has no such buffer; a judgment against her professional activities is a judgment against her personally.

The second reason is professional standing. Conducting business through an entity signals a degree of seriousness and infrastructure that operating in one's own name does not. Production companies, studios, and financiers are accustomed to dealing with entities. Wire instructions, tax forms, and contractual counterparties are cleaner when the writer is signing as a managing member of a clearly named company rather than as an individual. For writers who are also producing, who are accumulating multiple projects, or who are building toward a recognizable production banner, the entity becomes the vehicle through which a professional identity is constructed over time.

The third reason is tax flexibility. Depending on income level and the structure of the entity, an LLC can offer tax treatment that is more advantageous than sole proprietorship, for example, an LLC that elects to be taxed as an S corporation can, in some circumstances, reduce the writer's exposure to self-employment tax on a portion of her earnings. The specifics are highly fact-dependent, and the analysis requires actual numbers best determined by an accountant or CPA.

These benefits do not come without cost. Forming and maintaining an entity involves paperwork that the sole proprietor never has to think about. There are formation fees and, in many states, annual franchise taxes or filing fees that apply regardless of whether the entity earned anything that year. California, for example, imposes a minimum annual franchise tax on LLCs that operate in the state, and that obligation does not go away in a year when no projects close. There are separate bank accounts to maintain, separate books to keep, and separate tax returns to file. The administrative burden is real, and a writer whose professional income is modest and whose project volume is low may find that the cost and complexity of running an entity outweigh the benefits.

The tax consequences also cut in both directions. While the right entity structure can reduce certain tax obligations, the wrong one can increase them or can create complications that the writer did not anticipate. Loan-out corporations, for example, are common among more established writers but they introduce their own complexities around payroll, benefits, and the proper allocation of income between the entity and the individual.

The right answer for any individual writer requires a conversation with a certified public accountant or tax professional who can look at the writer's actual income, projected projects, state of residence, and long-term professional plans, and advise on whether and what kind of entity makes sense. It also typically requires a conversation with an attorney to handle the formation correctly and to ensure that the operating agreement, if there are multiple members, addresses ownership, decision-making, and dissolution in a way that protects everyone involved. The cost of those conversations is modest relative to the cost of getting the structure wrong, and they are appropriate to have at the point in a career when professional income becomes regular enough that the question is no longer hypothetical.

It should be noted that a creative's personal business LLC is distinct from what the industry refers to as a film or project LLC. The personal business LLC is the entity through which a writer or other creative conducts her ongoing professional activities, such as receiving writing fees, holding intellectual property she owns, paying business expenses, and accumulating projects over the course of a career. It is a long-term vehicle tied to the creative herself. A film LLC, by contrast, is a single-purpose entity or special purpose vehicle (SPV) formed for the production of one specific film or television project. It exists to receive investor capital, contract with cast and crew, hold the production insurance, own the negative and the resulting copyright in the finished film, and ultimately distribute proceeds back to its investors and profit participants.

When the project wraps and revenues are accounted for, the SPV is typically dissolved. A creative who is also producing her own project may end up forming both: her personal business LLC remains the long-term home of her creative work and writing income, while a separately formed SPV handles the financing and production of any specific project she takes into production. Running production capital through a personal business LLC or holding career-spanning intellectual property inside an SPV, defeats the liability, accounting separation, and ownership that each structure is designed to provide.

Becoming a WGA Member

For screenwriters working in film and television, joining the Writers Guild of America is one of the most consequential career decisions and, in most cases, it is not a choice the writer makes in but a consequence of selling or being hired to write a project for a signatory company. The WGA is the labor union representing writers in motion pictures, television, radio, and new media in the United States, divided geographically into WGA West (covering writers west of the Mississippi) and WGA East (covering writers east of it).

Membership is not open by application in the way that joining a professional association might be. Eligibility is earned through accumulating a defined number of "units of credit" (currently twenty-four units within a three-year period) by selling original material to, or being employed as a writer by, a company that is a signatory to the WGA Minimum Basic Agreement. Once the unit threshold is met, the writer becomes eligible to join and, upon joining, pays an initiation fee (currently around $2,500 for WGA West) along with ongoing quarterly dues calculated as a percentage of covered earnings.

The benefits of WGA membership are substantial and operate on two levels. On the contractual level, the Minimum Basic Agreement guarantees scale minimums for every category of writing service, a pension and health plan funded by employer contributions, residuals on the reuse and exploitation of covered work, separated rights in original material (including the right to write the first sequel and certain reserved publication and dramatic rights), credit determination through the WGA's arbitration process rather than producer discretion, and access to the guild's grievance and arbitration machinery if a signatory company fails to meet its obligations.

On the practical level, membership signals professional legitimacy to agents, managers, and buyers, opens access to the guild's script registration service, member events, mentorship programs, and writing groups, and places the writer inside a network of working professionals who understand the industry from the inside. The trade-off is the obligation to write only for signatory companies. For most career screenwriters, that trade-off is not only acceptable but desirable, since signatory status is itself a marker of a buyer worth working with.

The Attorney as Creative Ally

One of the most persistent misconceptions that creatives have is the idea that hiring an attorney is an adversarial act to the project at hand. Some may have a belief that introducing legal counsel into a negotiation signals distrust, poisons the creative relationship, and may cause the other party to walk away from a deal they would otherwise have made. However, sophisticated producers and studio executives deal with entertainment attorneys as a matter of professional routine. Their business affairs departments are staffed by attorneys. The agreements they send to writers were drafted by attorneys, reviewed by attorneys, and approved by attorneys. The idea that introducing your own attorney into that process is an aggressive act is simply untrue in the industry. And if someone tries to tell you otherwise, then take that as a red flag, either to their level of professionalism or misguidance.

An entertainment attorney is not merely someone who reviews contracts, but a strategic advisor who understands the market, knows the players, has seen the patterns, and can assess the specific agreement against the backdrop of comparable transactions. She can tell you when a provision is genuinely standard and when it is presented as standard while being, in practice, aggressive. She can identify the provisions that matter most in the specific context of your project and focus the negotiation on those, rather than treating every clause as equally important. The relationship with a knowledgeable entertainment attorney, developed over time and maintained throughout a career, can be one of the most valuable professional assets a writer can have.

Creative Freedom as the Destination

The script, book, or other creative work is only the beginning. The deal that follows, along with the terms you negotiate, the rights you retain, and the protections you insist on, determines whether that beginning leads somewhere lasting.

The intention of this book is to raise awareness of the legal and business layers of a creative's professional life. While it should not be considered legal advice, nor a substitute for an attorney-client relationship with counsel who knows your specific situation or project, this book hopefully has given you the vocabulary, the frameworks, and the analytical positioning to be a more informed participant in the transactions that will shape your career.

Now go forth and create.

ACKNOWLEDGMENTS

I'm often asked how I became an entertainment attorney. While the response could fill a whole book, the short answer is we eventually end up doing what we're meant to do in the world, that is, with the help of others. My first acknowledgment is to my parents who took me to the movies every Friday night. What a gift and privilege that was in hindsight. The theater will always hold a sweet nostalgia for me, not to mention 1980's and 90's romcoms, something my mom and I had in common.

As I got older, movies were therapy—provoking inspiration, change, and ideas that no other medium could. I ended up going to law school for the purpose of affording my life to be a fiction author one day. I'm still doing that, although swap fiction for non-fiction, for now.

My first legal job out of law school was clerking for The Honorable David Kennedy who encouraged me to write. And that I did, which resulted in a long resume of published legal journals. More importantly, it gave me the confidence to be a "writer." Thank you to the late Judge Kennedy for your vision.

For many years, I had a love-hate relationship with the practice of law, but that changed when I embraced the idea of working with creatives to help get their work out into the world. Justice Ruth Bader Ginsburg was an inspiration for my change of heart, along with the #metoo movement, all of which now seems like a fever dream.

To my wife, Rachel, thank you for the endless support—and for the enthusiastic snacks while I studied for the California Bar at an age not meant for such things.

And thank you to Maryann Russell who continues to remind me what I'm meant to do when I forget.

A special thanks to all the colleagues with whom I've had the honor and opportunity to practice this profession, and particular appreciation to Joshua Lastine, whose insight and practical perspective on entertainment law helped shape my early experience in the field.

Lastly, thank you to all the clients who entrusted me with their work and, in doing so, helped inspire my own path in the entertainment industry. This book is for you.

OTHER RESOURCES

Clearance & Copyright: Everything You Need to Know for Film, Television, and Other Creative Content by Michael Donaldson, Lisa Callif, et. al (5th Edition 2023)

Hollywood Dealmaking: Negotiating Rights and Talent Agreements for Film, TV, and Digital Media by Dina Appleton and Daniel Yankelevits (4th Edition 2025)

The Biz: The Basic Business, Legal and Financial Aspects of the Film Industry in a Digital World by Schuyler Moore (6th Edition 2023)

Dealmaking in the Film & Television Industry: From Negotiations to Final Contracts by Mark Litwak (2017)

Writing Treatments That Sell: Create and Market Your Story Ideas to the Motion Picture and TV Industry by Kenneth Atchity and Chi-Li Wong (2013)

The Business of Television by Ken Basin (2nd Edition 2024)

Influence: The Essential Guide to the Psychology of Influence and Persuasion in Everyday Life by Robert Cialdini (2014)

ABOUT THE AUTHOR

Tisha Morris, Esq. is an entertainment attorney and founder of Legacy Arts Law PC, dedicated to helping creative entrepreneurs build and protect their legacies in business and entertainment. Her clients include independent filmmakers, authors, publishers, production companies, and creative entrepreneurs building careers meant to last.

She is the bestselling author of five nonfiction books and has been featured on *Netflix, Law & Crime, ABC's Live with Kelly and Ryan, KTLA, KCAL, Today.com*, and *Elle Decor*. Tisha is an active member of the Beverly Hills Bar Association, California Lawyers for the Arts, Women in Film, and presents on legal panels at film festivals and industry events. Tisha lives in Ojai, CA, and can be found online at www.tishamorris.com.

Connect with Tisha at:
LinkedIn: @tishamorris
Instagram: @tishalmorris
TikTok: @tishalmorris
IMDb: @tishamorris

www.ingramcontent.com/pod-product-compliance
Lightning Source LLC
Chambersburg PA
CBHW011349230926
51848CB00003B/518